RIDING WITH THE GHOST

RIDING WITH THE GHOST

A Memoir

JUSTIN TAYLOR

RANDOM HOUSE | NEW YORK

Published in the United States by Random House,
an imprint and division of Penguin Random House LLC, New York.

RANDOM HOUSE and the HOUSE colophon
are registered trademarks of Penguin Random House LLC.

"Death of an Heir of Sorrows" was originally published as
"What It Means to Be Alive" in *Harper's* (June 2019).

Grateful acknowledgment is made to Secretly Canadian Publishing for
permission to reprint an excerpt from "I've Been Riding with the Ghost,"
lyrics by Jason Molina, published by Autumn Bird Songs (ASCAP)/Secretly
Canadian Publishing (ASCAP). Reprinted by permission.

Library of Congress Cataloging-in-Publication Data
Names: Taylor, Justin
Title: Riding with the ghost : a memoir / by Justin Taylor.
Description: First edition. | New York : Random House, [2020]
Identifiers: LCCN 2019041738 (print) | LCCN 2019041739 (ebook) |
ISBN 9780593129296 (hardcover) | ISBN 9780593129302 (ebook)
Subjects: LCSH: Taylor, Justin | Authors, American—21st century—
Biography. | Authors, American—21st century—Family
relationships. | Fathers and sons—United States.
Classification: LCC PS3620.A9466 Z46 2020 (print) |
LCC PS3620.A9466 (ebook) | DDC 813/.6—dc23
LC record available at https://lccn.loc.gov/2019041738
LC ebook record available at https://lccn.loc.gov/2019041739

Printed in the United States of America on acid-free paper

randomhousebooks.com

1 2 3 4 5 6 7 8 9

First Edition

Book design by Susan Turner

For my sister, Melanie

CONTENTS

PART I

Death of an Heir of Sorrows

My father had decided that he would end his life by throwing himself from the top of the parking garage at the Nashville airport, which he later told me had seemed like the best combination of convenience—that is, he could get there easily, and unnoticed—and sufficiency—that is, he was pretty sure it was tall enough to do the job. I never asked him what other venues he considered and rejected before settling on this plan. He probably did not actually use the word "best." It was Mother's Day, 2013.

The date was not chosen for its symbolism. If anything, it was a rare instance of inattentiveness, strikingly out of character for a man who, generally speaking, had always been acutely sensitive—if not always appropriately responsive—to the feelings of others. Even now I cannot quite believe that he would neglect to consider the shadow his action would cast over future Mother's Days for his mother, children, and ex-wife, with whom by this point he was no longer actively acrimonious, though certain wounds of course had not yet healed (and still haven't, and won't). It is impossible for me to imagine how he failed to grasp all this; how, as a matter of courtesy abetted by a desire to avoid further disgrace for his action, he didn't choose the day prior or the day after.

But then, it is not quite correct to say that he chose the day.

My father had been unemployed for a long time—my sister, six years my junior, has almost no memories of him as a workingman—and he had been sick with tremors that were later revealed, we think, to have been heralds of Parkinson's, though Parkinson's is what is often called "an exclusion diagnosis," which means one cannot test positive for it or know with total certainty that one has it; one can only present symptoms that strongly suggest it and, all other reasonable medical possibilities having been ruled out, proceed with treatment as though the diagnosis were definitive.

All this plus, naturally, the depression that had come with the divorce itself, which my parents had each done their share to precipitate, but which my father had not sought and did not accept.

He got a bit of money from the sale of the house and everyone thought he would move back near his parents, to the part of Florida where I grew up. When I say everyone thought that he would do this, what I mean is that we all wanted him to do this and thought that he would, because we wanted him to, and because we felt it was the inevitable next step and expected him to join us in this view, though we knew that such a move was without question the very last thing that he himself would ever want.

Instead of doing what we thought he would, he moved into a modest extended-stay hotel in Nashville, joined their rewards program, and sought to make his money last as long as he could. He had no other aim in mind, as far as I know, besides forestalling the inevitable, which my sister and I each understood to be his move back to Florida but which, at a certain point, we now understand, had come to mean, to him, his suicide.

He grew accustomed to eating no more than twice a day, often less. Smaller portions, cheaper restaurants. Takeout and hot bar. Burger King. Two bananas and a pear. He liked saving the money, wasn't hungry anyway.

It was unsettling, to say the very least, but who was going to lecture a grown man over the phone about how to eat?

He rarely saw my mother during this period, and though at times when they did interact—usually on the phone or via email—they bickered or rehashed old points of contention, it can be fairly said that she was not what kept him in that city. Certainly, he caused her no more trouble. I seem to recall that on one occasion she had to go to a doctor's appointment and be put under brief sedation there, and that he went with her and drove her home to the apartment she had, by this time, bought for herself.

She got some promotions at her job—the job that had brought the family to Nashville in the first place—and looked for better jobs with other companies, some in far-flung states, but didn't find one. Eventually she got a boyfriend, put her apartment on the market, moved in with him.

My father must have begun to hatch his plan when he realized he was coming to the end of his savings, but he always had a head for numbers and so it may not be correct to say that he "realized" where he stood, vis-à-vis the timeframe, since that suggests a gradual or dawning understanding, and he probably understood from the very beginning, immediately and completely, the story the numbers told, the timeline that they set—though he likely had to adjust the schedule to account for having joined the hotel's rewards program, the free nights he was accruing through it quite literally adding days to his life.

In any case, he decided, with what I'm sure was blazing anguish but which I prefer to imagine as a kind of icy calm— because imagining his misery is beyond me, or because it would be the easiest thing in the world—that when all of his money and rewards points were spent and gone, he would check out of the hotel, wait for night to fall, drive to the airport, park the car, and throw himself off the parking garage.

He had kept his phone off all day, and so had not called his mother for the holiday, which was unusual enough in itself that it was cause for family discussion by early afternoon. Then my sister, who was in law school in Washington, DC, checked her email and saw a note from him suggesting that his record collection—at this point still in storage at my mother's apartment, which she had not yet sold—might be worth some real money if she, my sister, ever cared to sell it. He was not perhaps as obscure as he meant to be, but then, for obvious reasons, he was in an agitated state and not paying his typically rigorous attention to language. My sister alerted the rest of the family and they all spent the day calling him, leaving increasingly urgent voicemails, sending him emails, doing anything they could, which wasn't much. My sister called the Nashville police and filed a missing-persons report.

I say that "they" did these things because even though my sister called me immediately, and I called my father immediately after that, leaving a message the contents of which I cannot recall and which, in fact, I can barely remember leaving—though I can see myself standing in the sunny home office in my old apartment, in Brooklyn, phone in hand, lips moving, like watching myself in a movie—I did not email him or call a second time. An enormous choking silence rose up in me and there was ice around my heart, which was filled with mourning, and there was ice, too, in my throat, so that to speak would have been to choke on ice. I went about my day more or less normally—my then-girlfriend (now wife) and I were looking, as it happened, for a new apartment—believing, in my ice-bound heart, that my father was already gone and trying to make sense of this and failing to do so and telling myself that it would become intelligible to me when the call of confirmation came. I thought of the last song on *Bright Flight,* my favorite Silver Jews record, and the line that goes, *"When I was summoned to the phone / I knew in my bones that you had died alone."* I thought, *I know what this means now.*

But that wasn't true.

My father sat in his parked car—my sister's old silver Nissan, which she gave him when she went to law school—on the top level of the parking garage at the airport, in the orange bath of a sodium lamp—or so I imagine—and for some reason turned his phone on for a moment before opening the driver's-side door. I don't know what he meant to see or who

7

he meant to contact, or if he meant to do something else entirely, but the profusion of missed calls and text messages that barraged him when his home screen loaded all had their intended effect—though not by virtue of their content, which he mostly never read or heard. The sheer number of them made him think that something bad must have happened to a member of the family, so he called my sister to find out what it was. She kept him on the phone for several hours. I have no idea how she did that, or what they said to each other, beyond that he confessed his intention and she talked him out of it, slowly and with unswerving persistence.

He ended up checking into a hotel by the airport on a credit card supplied by his nephew, our cousin, whom he had at times helped his older sister raise.

Fastidious, disciplined, and already unaccustomed to taking meals, my father had fasted, he later told me, for the twenty-four hours prior to his attempt. He had done this in order to avoid leaving a mess when he died. He seemed proud to have thought of this exigency. He had his own dignity in mind, of course, but also quite earnestly meant to make easier the experience of the various police and emergency and janitorial workers upon whose evening his plan could not help but intrude. But after he checked into the hotel by the airport he found himself, for the first time in months if not years, hungry.

Everything was closed, even room service.

He went to bed starving.

At 3:30 in the morning the alarm clock in his hotel room, which had been mistakenly left set by the previous guest, probably someone with a predawn flight to catch, went off.

He woke up screaming and could not get back to sleep. Still starving, he sat in the chair by the window, waiting for the sunrise he never expected to witness, while his hands were racked by tremors intensified by his hunger and the other stresses to which he had been—and was still being—subjected. *This*, I imagine him thinking, with a resignation beyond disgust, beyond horror, *is what it means to be alive*.

Hunger and aloneness and pain and shame.

And yet he chose it.

He chose, under these conditions, to stay alive.

A few days later, relocated from the airport hotel back to the modest extended-stay where he had been living (which our cousin was now paying for indefinitely), he sent an email to everyone apologizing for the trouble and worry that he had caused. My sister, noticing that I was not among the recipients, forwarded this letter to me. She was sure, she said, that I hadn't been left off the list on purpose. Our father had just endured the worst days of his life, indeed was still in the midst of them, and such a lapse ought to be both explicable and forgivable. That was true. Still, I asked him about it a while later, when things were calmer and he felt comfortable enough to have offered, without being prompted, some of the particulars relayed above, which of course I would have no other way of knowing, and would not have thought to ask him to share. But now we were talking about it and he was telling me things, and so I asked him about the letter. His answer made sense in its way. He said that everyone else had flooded him with communiqués, whereas I had only called him once. Since he hadn't, in the thick of things, listened to any of the voicemails, he thought it stood to reason that I had, obliviously and coincidentally, just called to say hello, or maybe to update him on my apartment search. It wasn't, he said, that I hadn't earned the apology—though as you can see by my own account, I clearly hadn't, and "earn" is a fraught word; he did not owe anyone an apology—it was only that I was better off for having been spared the ordeal. He didn't see the point, he said, in breaking what he'd understood to be my peace of mind by including me in what he'd meant, at that time, to be the final word on the terrible subject, though of course this, too, proved not to be the case, since now he wanted to talk about it.

We talked about it and talked about it, on this and other occasions, until his death, from complications of his illness, in 2017. Over time, he narrativized his experience—that is, made the story tellable, to himself and others—and as he did so it developed, as every story must, a shape, an arc. Small but vivid details, like the alarm clock in the hotel room, for instance, were deployed adroitly and exploited for narrative effect.

There was just one hole in my father's story, a small plot-level inconsistency that was there from the beginning and never got resolved. It's about the note. Not the second note, but the first one. The one he sent my sister.

I am, as I've said, six years older than my sister, and I am the son. My father's son. His only son, who by the way knows a hell of a lot more about records than my sister does. When we were growing up I used to play them whenever he would let me, which wasn't often. He has a mint-condition copy of

Sticky Fingers, first pressing with the real zipper, easily worth a few hundred bucks to the right buyer. Frank Zappa's *Freak Out.* Six or eight Beatles albums, nothing rare but all pristine. *Shakedown Street,* the Grateful Dead's bad foray into disco. The Eric Burdon and the Animals record with the little scratch on the track after "House of the Rising Sun" that he said I made and I said he did. *Band on the Run. A Night at the Opera. Leftover Wine,* the Melanie Safka live album. *Countdown to Ecstasy. Strange Days. In the Court of the Crimson King.*

He knew I might have sold a few of the collector's items, but no more than that. He knew I would have kept the collection and treasured it, whereas my sister, whatever else she might treasure, would tell you herself that when it comes to these old records, she couldn't give a shit. He knew that too.

So why didn't he send the note to me?

But of course I understand this. There is no hole, or there is but it's not in the story.

He knew that if he sent the note to me, I would not have deciphered it. If he had sent the note to me I would have been overmatched by its obscurity, imperfect as it was. Indeed when my sister first shared it and her concerns with me that day I told her she was making a big deal out of nothing. Some cryptic note about selling records. She had to convince me. And so if it had been left to me, my father's plan would have gone off without a hitch, and my sister would be telling me now and for the rest of our lives, dishonestly, that there was no way anyone could have read that note and known. I should be proud of him, or at least thankful, that he knew me well enough, that he had enough desire for life left in him, even then, to know not to trust me to save his.

What I said to my sister when we spoke on the phone that afternoon I still remember: "Oh, you know Dad," I said. "Dad's fine."

Belated Introduction

Lawrence Wayne Taylor. Larry, always Larry. Never Lawrence, and rarely Mr. Taylor. The only honorific he ever wore comfortably was in my and my sister's Little League days: "Coach." Born May 15, 1952, middle child and only son of George and Barbara. "Taylor" from the German "Schneider" from the Russian "Portnoy." George's father had emigrated from Russia as a teenager. He owned a barbershop on South Third and Keap Street, Brooklyn. George was born and raised in Williamsburg, where his neighborhood friends included Mel Brooks (or so he always claimed). Barbara was born in Poland and was gentry; she has vague memories of a house and servants, of being pulled to school on a sleigh. And pogroms. Her father came over in 1919 and sent for the family six years later, when Barbara was nine years old. She made passage aboard the *St. Louis*, the same ship that, in 1939, was turned back by President Roosevelt, dooming nearly eight hundred Jewish refugees to Hitler—the Ship of Fools.

Barbara and George met in Williamsburg, Brooklyn, and were married at eighteen and twenty years old, in 1943. It was a Wednesday-morning ceremony, performed in the rabbi's living room. George left soon after to serve in the Pacific theater. They had three children: Ronni in 1948, Larry in '52, and Francine in '59. They moved around Long Island a bit, but the kids grew up primarily in a town called Merrick. George, during most of these years, was a traveling salesman. Siding and kitchen knives were two of his steadiest products. Barbara was a full-time homemaker, but it was a difficult home to grow up in. "My parents didn't do 'kid things,'" Ronni told me once. "If they took us to the movies it was because they wanted to go to the movies, some movie they wanted to see and we were just there. Frankly, they didn't ever seem like they really liked having kids."

For people of that generation, and especially for Jews after the war, the question of whether to have children was no question at all. It was simply what you did after you got married, and so it seems entirely possible to me that George and Barbara *did* want children, though less out of any innate parental instinct than as part of the generational urge to resist our attempted eradication. And it may also have been the case that, as a first-/second-generation immigrant couple, they saw two or three children as part of the middle-class American life that they envisioned for themselves, a dream that ultimately eluded them. "They never had any money," Ronni told me. "They got by, but they never had anything."

My childhood memories of their home are of a place

where there was nothing for a kid to play with, where a certain silence prevailed, broken only by the occasional (inevitable) screaming match. In this regard, my experience was probably right in line with that of my father and my aunts when they were young.

In the spring of 1969, just after Larry finished his junior year of high school, the family moved to South Florida, which in those days was still a hopelessly Podunk place to live, especially for a teenager long accustomed to taking the train in from Long Island to Manhattan, alone or with friends, to see a baseball game or just to go exploring. I don't know why the Taylors moved to South Florida, though I assume it was for George's work. But I know that Larry hated it there. He told me countless times that he regarded the move as one of the major traumas of his life.

His hurt was compounded by the fact that a close friend's parents had offered to take him in for his senior year so that he could stay in Merrick and graduate with his class. He begged for permission to do this, and Barbara granted it. Here's the way he always told it to me: "I'd made all my arrangements, I'd told everyone I was staying, I was packed up. And she had *promised*." Then as the move date loomed, she changed her mind—or perhaps had never meant to let him stay to begin with and had simply told him that he could so he would stop asking. "She said to me, 'What are you, *stupid*, you think I'd let you do that? I never promised you anything.' Like none of it had ever happened."

Barbara also took the move as an opportunity to throw out several boxes of Larry's baseball cards and back issues of *Mad* magazine. He remembered the details on every lost card, and

15

when I went through my own card-collecting phase, in the early 1990s, he would sometimes browse my Beckett guide and muse over how many tens of thousands of dollars all that so-called junk was now worth. He was able to save about a shoebox's worth of cards, and one stack of issues of *Mad*. Characteristically, he kept both the cards and the magazines in mint condition. They sat at the back of the closet in the master bedroom of the house where I grew up. With the Beckett guide, we priced the cards that he had kept, and though they weren't worth what, say, the vanished Mantle rookie would have been, they were worth something. But he never sold them, ostensibly for fear that they might be worth more later; really because he couldn't bear to part with them. Eventually the baseball card market collapsed. The *Mad* magazines were never worth anything, except as a window into what had passed for avant-garde comedy on Long Island in the mid-1960s. When I was around ten or eleven years old, I read them all.

Larry may have hated Florida, but he made friends there, some of whom he stayed close with for long enough that I have memories of them: Zach and Sharlien, Marsha and Charlie, and Mark Starkman—who would in time become Larry's college roommate, and then my uncle. Before long he grew comfortable and (though he hated to admit it) came to think of South Florida as home.

In truth, it was his mother's betrayal that scarred him, not the fact of having to relocate. But he could not separate these ideas in his mind, and so for the rest of his life it was all but guaranteed that a lighthearted anecdote about adolescent hijinks in South Florida would, sooner or later, wend its way around to mourning for the lost paradise of Merrick, Long Island. This is a story I have heard a hundred if not a thousand times.

Larry graduated from high school in 1970. His parents thought college was pointless, a waste of money, and refused to help him pay for it. George wanted Larry to join the family business, though it's unclear what exactly this might have meant. The Taylors, during these years, got by (as Ronni once put it to me) on "this and that." For a while they had a table at the flea market, selling hunting knives, brass knuckles, and other random stuff you might find at a sporting-goods store or a pawnshop.

Larry lived at home, worked part-time, and put himself through Broward Community College. Around the time he finished his associate's degree, George had a heart attack and was unable to work for a year. Larry put school on hold and supported his parents and his younger sister, Francine, then in her teens, by getting a job in a door factory doing intense manual labor. Some days his job was to lift fire doors onto and off of a conveyor belt; other days he sprayed the fire-retardant polystyrene core into their hollow bodies with a hose.

Meryl and Mark Starkman had also been forcibly relocated to South Florida from New York (Rosedale, Queens), and their mother—my grandma Lorelei—took the move hard. Lorelei was inconsolable for years, writing several times a week to her sister back in New York, my great-aunt Ellen, detailing her hatred for Florida, while her husband worked long hours and the kids raised themselves. Meryl was an indifferent student but artistic: She could draw, paint, craft, and design and sew her own clothes. "It was just so hot in the high school," she told me once. "This huge concrete sweat shack that didn't have any air conditioning. You'd just fall asleep if you went there, so it was like, why even bother, you know?"

The Starkmans lived in Southwest Miami, an hour's drive from where Larry lived, in Hollywood. He was introduced to Mark through their mutual friend, Zach, whom Larry had known back in New York and reconnected with in Florida. Larry would drive down to see Zach because he didn't know anyone else. As it happened, Zach lived down the block from Mark and Meryl. Mark, Zach, and Larry became a tight-knit trio, the center of a group that Meryl remembers now as simply "the guys." "They hung out at each other's houses, including ours, so that's how I came to know them. This would have been '72 and '73. Me and some of my friends, we were sophomores or juniors then, and we started hanging out with the guys, who were mostly undergrads at either University of Miami, Miami Dade Community College, or Broward Community."

Even though he'd dropped out of school to work at the door factory, Larry found time to tutor Meryl in math. It was a working-class romance, like something out of a Springsteen song. As a reward for passing a difficult test, he took her to see the movie *Cabaret*, which he later came to describe as their first date. Meryl, however, is a bit more equivocal: "We weren't seeing each other exclusively, but we must have been seeing each other somewhat regularly, and it progressed."

Mark had skipped a grade in high school, and so by this time he was finishing his BA. He applied to law school at the University of Florida and was accepted. With George healthy enough to work again, Larry was able to return to school.

He applied to UF as an undergraduate and Mark and Larry moved to Gainesville together in the fall of 1973. Meryl finished high school in 1974 and was accepted to the Fashion Institute of Technology, which took her back north to New York City for the 1974–75 school year. She visited Larry and Mark at UF before she left, and Larry visited her a few times while she was in New York. They were on and off during this time, and each dated other people, though in later years he preferred not to acknowledge the break (or whatever it was), focusing instead on the eighteen-hour drives he'd taken to New York as proof of his dedication—how he hadn't stopped to eat or sleep. He hadn't stopped for anything but gas.

He studied business and completed his BA in 1975. He applied to the law school but was not admitted, so he moved back to South Florida and into his parents' house. Meryl decided to transfer from FIT to Miami-Dade Community College for the second year of her associate's degree, at least in part to be with him, though instead of moving in together, she too moved back in with her parents. "I was planning to go back to Florida after school," she told me. "So why not finish there? It made sense to me. But I had no idea at the time that FIT was such a superior school, or what a degree in fashion from MDCC would mean."

Larry had an artistic streak himself. He liked to read and was an eloquent writer. He didn't have spare credits (or tuition money) to spend on electives at UF, but he somehow squeezed in an introduction to photography course. He loved everything about it, from theories of composition to geeking out over gear, from working in the darkroom to the magic of seeing a personal vision turn into something tangible that you could share. It was his all-time favorite college experience and made him into a lifelong shutterbug.

Though he never learned to play an instrument, he loved listening to music and going to concerts. He saw a lot of shows at Pirates World, a theme park that had opened in Dania, Florida, in 1967. Pirates World had always staged occasional concerts, but in 1971—when Larry was nineteen years old and still living in nearby Hollywood—they started booking rock bands in earnest. (They were attempting to compensate for revenue lost to a certain mouse-mascotted park that had just opened in Orlando and drawn away their customer base.) I know that Larry saw Wishbone Ash, Three Dog Night, Ten Years After, the Moody Blues, Humble Pie, and the Guess Who, all of whom played that year. I wouldn't be surprised if he also caught Deep Purple, Jethro Tull, and Emerson, Lake & Palmer. Pirates World went out of business in 1975.

A born skeptic and typically a reflexive cynic, Larry nevertheless had a childlike awe, maybe even a religious reverence, for the strange combination of abandon and control that allowed a charismatic singer to draw and manipulate the attention of an audience, to serve as both its leader and its avatar, facilitating an experience that was at once individual and collective. It was incredible to him that some stranger's lyrics could speak not just *for* you but *through* you and maybe *as* you; how you could throw your whole self—voice box and consciousness, body and spirit—into this totally other person, the one who was on the stage or your home stereo or your car speakers, and lose yourself in the music, and then, at the far end of all that otherness, somehow find yourself, more truly and more strange.

This is an admittedly grandiose—indeed, borderline delusional—way to describe a crowd of '70s teens hollering along to "American Woman" or "Aqualung." And yet it's what Larry felt, at least some of the time; often enough to keep him coming back for more. He craved that catharsis, even if in some ways it scared him as much as it exhilarated him. He sometimes wondered what it would be like to be the singer on the stage instead of one of the thousand people singing along in the crowd. But that wasn't going to be his life, and he knew it. He wanted something stable and lucrative, white-collar, so he wouldn't struggle the way his parents always had. The law had been his first choice, but he took the rejection from UF's law school as definitive, and never reapplied there or anywhere else. He decided to become a stockbroker.

Meryl and Larry got married in 1977. They bought a one-bedroom condo in a new apartment complex that Meryl's father's company had had a hand in building. Among their new neighbors was another young married couple: Norman and Jeanette, who were practicing Modern Orthodox Jews. Meryl had not grown up in a remotely religious household, but her brother had been bar mitzvahed and she'd been part of the Jewish youth organization B'nai B'rith. The Taylors hadn't been religious either, but they kept up some of the traditions and customs: They cleansed the house for Passover and held a seder, which George led; they went to services at the high holidays and fasted on Yom Kippur. Like Mark, Larry had been bar mitzvahed. Jeanette's religiosity was therefore neither wholly foreign nor familiar to Larry and Meryl, but it intrigued them. They began to explore their heritage as a living thing: a faith practice. I'm not sure that they were "believers" in the most literal sense of the word (they did not, for instance, join a synagogue or refrain from work on the Sabbath), but they got in the habit of lighting the Shabbat candles before Friday-night dinner and for nearly three years they kept a kosher home, with separate sets of dishes for milk and meat, and a separate set of separate sets of dishes just for Passover.

"We were curious, and it was really interesting," Meryl told me. "To learn how to do all this, and what it's supposed to mean." The spell was broken, ironically enough, by a visit from Jeanette's mother, who refused to eat off of Meryl and Larry's dishes, because they had been "made kosher" through ritual purification (and ten cycles in the dishwasher) but had not been "originally kosher." As she served this woman dinner on a paper plate, Meryl realized that she was never going to be Jewish enough in some people's eyes no matter what she did, and that these rules didn't make sense anyway, which meant that all the hassle was for nothing. *Four* sets of dishes for *two* people? They moved on from Judaism to health food, traded prayers and candles for tofu and carob. Before long, they got tired of that too.

Dad's older sister, Ronni, had gotten married in 1969 and moved to Richmond, Virginia, for her husband, Bill, to attend medical school. Ronni gave birth to her first son, Michael, in 1973, and her second son, Adam, in 1974. The marriage soured and Ronni moved to Florida permanently the same year that Meryl and Larry wed. Michael and Adam would have been four and three years old. There are boxes' worth of photographs, slides, and home video memorializing the time that my parents spent with their nephews throughout the late '70s and early '80s. "My kids *definitely* regarded Larry as a father figure," Ronni told me. I know that he regarded himself the same way.

Spending time with the boys made him feel needed and useful. He had a lot of love to give, and though I'm not sure whether he knew it (he certainly wouldn't have said it the way I'm about to say it), he was a person who needed to receive a lot of love as well. He cherished every trip to the park and the video arcade or the movies or the water slide, relished every baseball thrown and math worksheet agonized over. This is one reason why I wasn't born until 1982, though my mother has also told me that for a long time Dad hesitated to start a family. He feared repeating the mistakes his own parents had made, and he was worried about money. I believe he was also worried about shirking his obligation to Michael and Adam. What if they felt abandoned? What if he didn't have time for them anymore? I don't have concrete proof of this, but my theory is corroborated by something my mother said when I asked her about the six-year age gap between me and my sister, Melanie.

"Dad was scared to divide his attention. His own parents

were so unloving, such cold people, just totally uninterested in their children. He always swore he would never be like that, and he wasn't. He told you he loved you all the time and he always took your concerns very seriously, a lot more seriously, to be honest, than we maybe should have. We were the parents, but you always got to have an opinion and sometimes a vote, and most families just don't work that way. He loved you so much he worried he would love another kid less, or that if he didn't then that meant he'd have to love you less. It was very hard for him to see that he'd just have more love and attention to give, even though we both had always planned on two if not three kids. He kept saying, 'I'm not done with this one yet.' Kidding, of course, but also not. He probably would have kept hesitating forever and you'd have been an only child but I finally put my foot down."

Throughout the late '70s and early '80s Meryl had worked in garment factories in Hialeah, making use of her skill as a clothing designer while Larry tried to establish himself as a stockbroker. It didn't go well. He had an incredible head for numbers and an intuitively sophisticated grasp of the market; the only problem—as literally everyone who ever knew him seems to have warned him—was that his quick temper made him ill suited to a profession based on glad-handing and schmoozing. He had no personal Rolodex on which to draw and wasn't good at showing deference to his bosses either.

The first office that hired and trained him closed shortly

after he started working. He was reassigned to another office within the company, but was let go shortly thereafter, in part because he refused to promote the subpar stocks that the company wanted the brokers to push to their clients, which meant he was always at loggerheads with his manager. He tried selling insurance; he dabbled in Amway. His in-laws offered to pay for night school if he wanted to study law after all: He said no. In August 1979 he applied to the management training program at 7-Eleven. Though rated a "satisfactory candidate," he never worked for 7-Eleven, so the only reason I know this is because he kept a copy of his personnel-evaluation form, which is downright disturbing in its accuracy, which may be why he kept it.

SUMMARY ASSESSMENT: Mr. Taylor is very bright. He is assertive and competitive. He is a reflective and in-depth thinker. He enjoys analyzing problems. However, he should not over-analyze them at the expense of timely actions. He tends to be overly critical of people in general. He may have difficulty working cooperatively and he can be quite disagreeable when he wants to be.

After I was born, my parents decided that Mom would stay at home. When I was five or six months old, Mom had lunch with another young mother, who mentioned that there was a lot of film and fashion work going on in South Florida, and they were always looking for new faces, especially for children's clothing catalogs. Her son, just shy of a year old, was making decent money, and sometimes they even let him keep the clothes! She gave my mom the name of a couple of talent agents.

Because babies grow and change so fast, there's no sense taking formal headshots of them. Dad, eager to put his photography skills to use, took pictures of Mom holding me, and they sent them to the agents. I began to book work right away, but one of the agents also noticed Mom. She wasn't interested in acting or modeling, but the family's finances were in such rough shape she figured she might as well give it a shot. She ended up as a recurring extra on *Miami Vice*, the back of a head in Crockett and Tubbs's office. Occasionally, she played other roles: a pregnant corpse at the city morgue, for example. She was on the show for four of its five seasons.

I have a few muddled memories of the *Miami Vice* set from the mid-'80s: the craft services tent, a Christmas party. Mom says Philip Michael Thomas was a friendly guy, and that Don Johnson wasn't. She once spent a day on a boat with Frank Zappa, who was playing a drug dealer; he was seasick the entire shoot.

Mom's acting career started and ended with *Miami Vice*, but mine was longer lived. I loved attention and was loud and energetic, always happy to ham it up. Because I was an early and avid reader it was easy for me to memorize dialogue, often the single biggest problem when it comes to working with young performers. I did print, radio, and television commercials. My first and probably biggest TV success was a commercial for the Florida Citrus Growers Association, shot when I was in first grade. In it, another little boy and I are in a school cafeteria negotiating a trade for my very desirable thermos of orange juice. He offers some of his sandwich, then a doughnut, which I finally agree to take in exchange for *half* the orange juice. He takes the thermos and drinks the whole thing. I say, "Hey, you drank more than half!" He says, "I had to, my half was on the bottom!" This commercial ran nationwide for at least a year, and in Florida for longer than that.

At my agent's urging, my mother and I spent the summer of 1992 in New York, so that I could pursue bigger roles. We lived with my mother's aunt and uncle, Ellen and Henry, in their house in Baldwin, Long Island. Every day Mom and I took the LIRR into Manhattan so I could go on auditions, sometimes two or three in a day. This was the summer I turned ten years old. My father and my sister (who was three years old at the time) stayed behind in Florida, because it would have been impossible to put us all up at Ellen's house, and because Dad—who had found his place in his industry, and was working as a stockbroker—was the sole breadwinner. Splitting up the family, even temporarily, put a lot of pressure on my parents' relationship, as well as on their roles as parents. They were each, in effect, single-parenting: Mom navigating the New York City casting scene while Dad worked in an office all day, then rushed off to pick up his toddler from his in-laws or the sitter. This wasn't what they had imagined for their marriage, but here was this huge opportunity— right? It seemed foolish to let their son's big chance slip by.

There were a few close calls with success, most notably a lead role in *Conversations with My Father,* a play about first-generation Jews assimilating as Americans after the war. The play would premiere on Broadway, be a finalist for the

Pulitzer Prize for Drama, and win Judd Hirsch a Tony Award. When I got the callback for it, instead of being excited I was terrified. Not about memorizing the lines or performing live, but about having to stay in New York all through the fall, away from my friends, and with the family divided indefinitely on my behalf. I did my best at the audition, but was relieved when I didn't get the part, which in the end went to some kid named Jason Biggs. (The other big callback was for the movie *The Good Son,* the role that ultimately went to Elijah Wood.) I booked nothing that summer, but the experience proved important for an entirely unrelated reason.

Mom had suggested that I keep a diary while we were in New York. I did, and continued to keep it intermittently for the year that followed. It was largely a list of desserts consumed, toys acquired, and tourist attractions visited, but there were passages where I wrote about how I was feeling: happy, sad, homesick, confused about whether I should keep trying to act. The diary doesn't contain any big revelations, and I'm not sure whether it's still extant. (I've seen it as an adult, but not recently; it may have been misplaced or thrown away.) Its real value, I now believe, was to help me develop a writing habit. By the middle of fifth grade I had lost interest in diary-keeping but was writing stories that ran the gamut from Stephen King–inspired monster-and-vampire fare to more realist riffs on friends and school; I even attempted poetry! I took this work seriously and it became something I was willing to prioritize and make time for. I can only imagine how strange it must have been for my parents when their eleven-year-old started talking about his writing hobby as "work," but they were never anything less than encouraging and supportive.

That said, there were a lot of fights about my conviction that this work was more important than, say, the homework I got at school, or getting a full night's sleep. By the time I finished elementary school I had what could earnestly be described as a writing practice.

My acting career, meanwhile, had stalled. I became increasingly ambivalent about the enterprise, and there was the unavoidable fact that puberty was not being especially generous to me. Being able to memorize dialogue was no longer the impressive feat it had once been. I didn't want to take acting classes or go out to LA for pilot season, and becoming a teen heartthrob didn't seem to be in the cards. I got asked to audition less and less often, and that was fine with me, though when a call did come, I still went, if only for the chance to make some money.

The last commercial I did was in 1996, for the debut of a new roller coaster called the Mantis at the Cedar Point amusement park in Sandusky, Ohio. The commercial was shot in two parts. The first part was shot in South Florida. The camera sits at bug's-eye view in the grass and I hold my foot above it, threatening to squish. "Should I or shouldn't I?" I sneer at the bug. "Ever wonder why you're not supposed to step on a mantis?" the announcer asks teasingly as the screen cuts to black. (You can find both parts of the Mantis commercial on YouTube; if the orange juice commercial exists anywhere online, I have not been able to locate it.)

For the second part of the commercial, they flew Dad and me out to Cedar Point and I spent twelve hours riding the Mantis. It was early spring and bitterly cold. Part one of the commercial had been running for weeks already. (My wife, who grew up in Michigan, remembers seeing it on TV.) As we walked around the theme park I saw people doing impressions of me, raising a foot up and shouting, "Should I or shouldn't I?" to their friends. My reaction to this was mixed: It was cool, but also weird, and not entirely welcome. But Dad was unequivocal in his excitement. He was impressed. He was *proud*. He wanted me to walk up to people and introduce myself. "Meet your fans," he said. I wouldn't.

There's no question that Dad found some vicarious satisfaction in my fame (such as it was), but the money was also a major motivation. A few hundred bucks here or a few thousand there was a lot for us in those days, and though there were times when the family probably could have used that money, they didn't take it. When I booked a commercial or got an unexpected residual check, I was typically allowed to spend some small portion of my earnings on something I wanted—toys, later books and video games—and then the rest was put away for college. I knew all this at the time, but money and college are pretty abstract concepts to an eighth grader whose main concern is not embarrassing himself in front of strangers. After the Mantis, I decided I was done.

For ten solid years, from the mid-'80s to the mid-'90s, Dad was a broker at a firm called Corporate Securities Group. At one point they tapped him to open and manage a new branch office. The story of how and why this fell apart is convoluted, probably not worth telling even if I could do it justice, which I can't. Basically he had a massive falling-out with a few people in his office, possibly in the course of attempting to expose some kind of malfeasance or fraud that was going on in-house. At a guess, I'd say he was correct on whatever business decision or question of ethics instigated the conflict, but that he became so aggressive and implacable with his colleagues and superiors that he lost any moral high ground he might have had, and gave his enemies all the ammunition they needed to protect themselves and take him out. It's likely that his presence, rather than the issue he raised, came to be viewed as the primary liability in the office.

When Larry Taylor flew off the handle, he flew all the way off, and there was never any telling how long it would last or what the consequences would be. His life—our lives—were marked by these outbursts: ejections from ball games, restaurants where we were no longer welcome, broken friendships, screaming matches followed by days of silence. He was often Billy Joel's "Angry Young Man" ("with his foot in his mouth and his heart in his hand"), a song he loved and occasionally quoted, usually in the context of an apology. He would insist—despite all available evidence—that he was *no longer* the self-destructive hothead Joel describes.

For what it's worth, his apologies were always sincerely offered because his remorse was always real. Among family and close friends these apologies were usually accepted, though forgiveness could hardly erase the memory of what had been said in the heat of an argument, or the scorch of the heat itself. But with colleagues and bosses, of course, it was an entirely different story. He was, again per Joel, "proud of his scars and the battles he's lost," but he was running out of battles to fight. And he was no longer young.

The last year at Corporate Securities Group was disastrous for him and for our family. He ended up with no job and powerful enemies within the industry. His career never recovered.

During my last few years of high school he was home a lot, and then he was home all the time. He kept a stock-tracking program open on the family computer and CNBC blared all day from the living-room TV, but I understood at some level that whatever he was doing, it was not actually work. My parents fought more and more often about money.

Dad and I fought too, bitterly, over ludicrously minor things. Thrift-store shopping, for instance, enraged him. He found it offensive and insulting that while most of the guys I'd grown up with were wearing Tommy and Polo, I elected instead to "dress like a homeless person in other people's garbage." When I wanted a chain wallet, he said only criminals and bikers wore them. Eventually I was allowed to get a small chain, but then I upgraded myself to a much longer, heavier one—it was actually a dog collar, purchased not at Pacific Sunwear or Hot Topic but in the pet aisle of a Walgreens. I can still hear the fury in his voice, see the anger in his eyes, when he caught me with it.

A lot of this had to do with class. I understood myself as engaged in a rebellion against the stultifying suburban values all around me, whereas my parents understood themselves as trying desperately to present a facade of middle-class stability that was always just out of reach. If I'd understood this at the time, I would have better understood Dad's sensitivity to my presenting myself as being as poor as we actually were. (That said, this was the '90s, and pretty much anyone who wasn't dressed like a Backstreet Boy or a Young Republican was dressed like Kurt Cobain.)

We had the requisite confrontation over drug use, though the way this archetypical moment played out was highly unusual. I've never met anyone else with a story quite like mine, and I think it says something about who my father was, and what our relationship was like.

I started smoking pot in tenth grade, and my parents caught on pretty quickly. Mom didn't think it was a huge deal, but Dad, who abstained from all substance use (from hard drugs and alcohol to caffeine and Tylenol), thought it was a very big problem. He was worried about gateway drugs, overdosing, a life of crime—the whole DARE checklist. And yet his respect for my privacy was so absolute that he would not search my room, reeking as it was. Instead he took me out to breakfast one Saturday morning, itself such an unusual occurrence that I knew he must want to have a Serious Conversation. Given how little he'd been working in the past year, and how strained my parents' relationship had become as the financial pressures mounted, I assumed that he was going to tell me they were getting divorced. We wound up at the mall food court, where I ordered a plate of bourbon chicken (at ten-thirty in the morning!), and he, characteristically, decided he wasn't hungry after all. I sat there eating sickly sweet chicken, growing increasingly baffled as he laid out all of his circumstantial evidence of my pot use, and explained that it *was* circumstantial because he hadn't actually gone through any of my stuff. I was so relieved that this wasn't the Divorce Talk that I admitted he was right. But I told him that, if he himself believed everything he'd just said about the dangers and risks, then it was insane that he'd let me keep going for months while he gathered his evidence and harbored his suspicions. If this stuff was as bad as he claimed, why hadn't he prioritized my safety over my privacy and raided my room right away?

He conceded the point. You might be surprised to hear that, but I wasn't. Dad could be impossible when he was in a rage, but he was fully capable of a good-faith debate, and was willing to admit when he changed his mind.

As it happened, I didn't find pot to be particularly enjoyable. It tended to leave me bored and boring, usually asleep before too long. By the time he'd confronted me I had lost most of the limited interest I'd had in the drug, and I told him that too. He believed me, I think in part because it was pretty close to his own experience with marijuana, though he didn't come out and say so at the time. I told him, again honestly, that there was still some pot in the house and that I would get rid of it. He said that sounded fine. I finished my chicken and we left the mall. The subject was never broached again.

I graduated from high school in 2000 and left for the University of Florida's summer session a few weeks later. In 2003, my mother lost her job in Miami and was recruited by a company out of Nashville. At my father's insistence, she moved there by herself to take the lay of the land before relocating the family. About a year later, after much stalling and negotiation, they sold the house in Miami and bought a place in a suburb of Nashville.

My father and sister joined my mother in the summer of 2004, between Melanie's sophomore and junior years of high school. She was inconsolable and so was Dad: The scenario was an almost exact repetition of what had happened to him when he was her age, and it signified for him a sort of ultimate failure. The two of them fed each other's sorrow, anger, and depression. I spent the summer of 2004 at the Nashville house also, helping them get settled and killing time. I had graduated from UF that spring, and come the fall I was headed for an internship at a magazine in New York City.

The misery in the air was palpable. Mom and I gamely attempted to get to know the area: We toured Civil War battlefields and the Jack Daniel's distillery, saw Ralph Stanley at the Grand Ole Opry. For the most part, Dad refused to participate in any of this, though there was one particularly ill-fated family excursion to a kitschy motel-turned-restaurant called the Loveless Cafe. I remember it as a decent if unexceptional meal for which we'd waited perhaps forty-five minutes longer than we ought to have. Dad thought it exemplified everything wrong with Tennessee, and mocked my mother mercilessly for having brought us there. Later, he made what he thought was a very funny PowerPoint presentation about how shitty it was and what a bunch of asshole rednecks Tennesseans are, and shared this document with his personal mailing list, an assortment of friends and family to whom he sent occasional (sometimes more than occasional) missives and screeds. The main thing I remember thinking that summer was that something was going to have to give, that there was simply no way things could keep on the way they were going. I figured Dad would, however grudgingly, acclimate to the situation. It was neither the first nor the last time that I made this particular mistake.

I spent the fall of 2004 in New York City, and the spring of 2005 in Portland, Oregon, living with some college friends who had moved there. I went back to Tennessee that summer and found things about the same as they'd been the year before—that is, grim. I left for New York again in September, to start my MFA. I ended up staying in New York for a decade and never lived in the Tennessee house again. I visited, of course, and was in regular contact with everyone. There was no point at which I would have described myself as estranged from my father, or vice versa. Our relationship remained intense, difficult, and close. But as his situation worsened, his behavior became more erratic, swerving between a depressive catatonia and an aggression that, even by his own standards, was troubling. He was aware that he was in an unhealthy mental state, but adamant—as always—in his refusal to admit there was a problem or accept any kind of help. Melanie finished high school in 2006 and she, too, left for UF.

After a particularly difficult visit to Nashville in early 2007, I decided to write my father a letter. I was neither subtle nor gentle. For the subject line, I just wrote "Letter." I won't quote the whole thing.

There's something I wanted to say to you while I was home, and you need to hear it. I'm really fucking worried about you. All day, every day. Twice in the past two weeks I've had to remind you that you're still on this side of the grave, and frankly you didn't sound especially convinced either time. I don't like the tone I'm taking right now, but I can't imagine another one that would get and hold your attention, so if it's any consolation I'm as uncomfortable with this as I hope you are. This family loves its silences, but I'm not playing that way anymore. [. . .] I'm not spending the rest of *my* goddamn life wondering what might have been different if I'd only said something.

He wrote me back the next day. His letter was easily ten times as long as the one I sent him, and covered a range of topics, as indeed my own letter had, but he ignored entirely the issue of his own health and well-being, so when I wrote back to him, I doubled down.

My reply wasn't nearly as long as his, not half as long as his, but it was long. Here's a chunk of it:

At no point did you address my main concern. So I will try to be even blunter than before: You seem to have become a kind of hermit, and spend most of your time in loathe of a world you will not participate in. I am concerned for your physical and psychological well-being. Though not a drunk or an addict, and not diseased, there is something going on in you that I would describe as a "condition" in any situation where I was an observer and not a participant. I am no longer willing to pretend that it isn't happening. It is. You have all my love and support, now and for ever, but I would feel a lot better if I knew that you were taking steps toward obtaining diagnosis, treatment, et al.

This thing—whatever it was—that *I* had started was not going the way that I had hoped it would. The conversation had slipped out of my control immediately, or maybe it had been a delusion on my part to think I'd ever had control of it to begin with. I'd framed my first letter as a sort of tough love, but it was obvious, looking over what I'd actually written and the way that I responded to his response, that I was furious with him. There was a part of me that did not care, in those moments, whether I ever spoke to him again or if I ended up making him hate me. Was that, subconsciously, what had motivated me to initiate this conversation? While it is technically true to say that this wasn't going how I'd hoped, it was going exactly the way that I would have anticipated, if I had bothered to think it through before diving in.

Three days after I sent my response, a package arrived in Nashville. It was a galley of an anthology of short fiction that I had spent the last year editing, to be published in early June 2007, just after I graduated from the MFA program. Though my first book of my own fiction was still three years away, this was a book and it had my name on it. On the cover, on the spine. I had been paid to produce it. The book was the biggest thing that had ever happened to me in my writing career (indeed it felt like the thing that gave me license to take the word "career" out of scare quotes) and it had a dedication page that read:

for my parents, who read to me

Dad sent me an email, which I *will* quote in full:

i just got home and took in the mail. there was a big envelope from you. i guessed it was the book and was quite excited to see it. i got to a page that has only seven words on it. i won't repeat them because i'm sure you know exactly what they are. i would say you don't know how much it means to me for us to be so acknowledged but i think you know exactly how much and that is likely one of the reasons the page exists. finding that page and the love, respect and honor i believe it conveys is a life's moment that makes many of life's not so rich moments pale and fade. thank you for providing it. i love you. your mother isn't home but i'll speak on her behalf and say she does too.

The other letters were never spoken of again. Their details grew vague and hazy in my mind. The next time I read them was almost exactly ten years later: January 2017. I had just arrived in Indianapolis for a teaching fellowship and was finding myself driven by a desire I did not yet understand (or, frankly, trust) to start taking some notes about my father. His physical and mental health were rapidly deteriorating and I wanted to document what was happening to him, as well as my thoughts and feelings about it. I began to write like I had that summer in New York when I was ten years old. This got me thinking about my childhood—and his. As I wrote what I remembered, the seemingly settled past began to revise itself in light of the unfolding, unraveling present.

Sitting alone in my little room in Indianapolis, reading these letters for the first time since we'd exchanged them, the main thing that surprised me was that I had been able to see and articulate the situation so clearly so early on. Everything I'd said then was true, and it had gotten worse, exponentially worse, over the next ten years. The letter in which I called him "a kind of hermit" read like a lost prophecy. If you'd asked me at any point before I reread these letters, I'd have told you that this wasn't something I knew yet, or that I possibly could have known way back in the first week of 2007. I would have told you that I'd learned these things—learned to think of him this way—only slowly, over the brutal decade that was to follow. But it wasn't true. It isn't true. All the hard-won wisdom that I've been telling myself was earned in the heat of crisis and the long simmer of misery, it turns out I knew all along.

This book, then, is an attempt to tell the story of those ten years, but also to deconstruct it. What were the stories my father told himself, and did I—do I—believe them? What are the stories I told myself about him or about us, and why did I—and do I still—believe those? If my father, as he often said during what turned out to be the last years of his life, was a failure, when and why did this failure occur? Did he fail all of us, or only himself? In what ways did we—did I—fail him? How did it come to that night on the roof of the airport parking garage, and what was the path back out? Who *was* Larry Taylor? It took me longer than it should have to realize that this last question was another way of asking, *Who am I?*

Indianapolis Notebook

I'm living in Indianapolis for the semester on a teaching fellowship. It's the end of January 2017. I flew into Nashville a few days ago and picked up a Volkswagen Passat that belongs to my mom's friend's kid, who is studying abroad for a year. I feel incredibly lucky that this came through for me, because the four or five grand it would have cost to rent a car for the semester is pretty much what I hope to have left over after taxes, living expenses, and my half of the rent on the apartment back in Portland. If not for the gift of this free car, this "writer-in-residence" position would be, essentially, a break-even deal.

I call Dad to check up. "How's it going?" I ask.

"I was sitting by the edge of the bed, something about sitting there, it's one of the only places—relief, a little relief, this was a week ago, and I've been afraid since then, afraid to sit there. One of the few things that was working and I lost it. I'm afraid now. I was sitting on the edge of the bed and I put my foot down. It came down wrong on the floor and it twisted. I rolled the ankle, I slipped. I fell. I fell between the edge of the bed and the desk. You know the room, you can picture where. I fell and hurt my ankle but I was also stuck at this angle, I lifted my arms to try to grab the edge of the desk, I couldn't reach it, then I did but I couldn't hold on, then I did hold on but my arms locked. I had no strength to lift myself up but now I could not let go, I was stuck that way, my muscles were exhausted, the pain I can't even tell you, the pain and shaking still this whole time, my body, so the back of my head, my neck, banging the leg of the desk, it's still bruised back there, my head my leg, I was drooling, crying, an hour and forty minutes, the feeling came back and I could move some, I got out of there but I haven't sat at the edge of the bed again, I'm afraid, but why afraid, I don't know, I mean I know but what I mean is when I was stuck there, that whole hour forty minutes all I thought about was starving to death, how I could starve to death there, and all I kept thinking was I wouldn't mind, I'm sorry I'm telling you this, if it only didn't take so long, if it could happen and be done already I really think I would say okay, fine."

"This was a week ago? Have you been to the doctor? Did Ronni or Fran come over?"

"I didn't call them. I didn't call anyone. I didn't tell anyone. I'm only telling you now because you asked how things are going. Well, that's how."

———

My sister and I talk on the phone. I tell her Dad's story.

"Seems like we'd better go down there, right?"

"Yeah."

He takes pills that relieve his shaking—now a relentless full-body tremor—for ninety minutes at a time, though sometimes they don't last quite that long and sometimes they fail to kick in at all, leaving him watching the clock for hours, shaking and waiting, because he can only take them three times a day. The pills' efficacy has diminished over time, but the daily maximum dose cannot be increased. He is without insurance and still too young for Medicare, so we cannot pay for him to try the other pills the current doctor says might work better. They cost upward of $1,000 a month. We've suggested putting up the money for a month's worth, just to see if they work, but he says this is pointless. It would be worse, he says, to know that something better was out there, and anyway what if they don't work, and that's another thousand bucks gone up in smoke?

It remains a remote but real possibility, even now, that he does not have Parkinson's. The first neurologist he saw, back in 2007, told him his shaking (then a barely noticeable tic) was a reaction to stress. He clung to this explanation for years, because he thought it meant he could blame his condition on the divorce. Of course, the diagnoses are not mutually exclusive: He may have Parkinson's, but it may have been triggered or at least accelerated by his emotional distress. Which is to say it is possible that he thought himself into this hell. It is not possible for him to think himself back out.

He lives alone in the apartment that his nephew Michael bought for him in Sunrise, Florida, not long after the suicide attempt in 2013. It's a small one-bedroom in a development near his sisters and his parents. My sister and I pay the maintenance and dues on it, a fact of which he is unaware. When he was young, he and his friend Steve used to drive past this development and joke to each other that no matter how far they fell in their lives, they'd only know they hit bottom if they ended up there. In fact, there are far worse places to live than the Sunrise Lakes Apartments, which are modest—even a little shabby—but basically comfortable. Still, the place was for them the very incarnation of failure. Now they both live there. Steve lives with his ailing father, who at some point a few years back took out a reverse mortgage on the apartment, so whenever he dies Steve will become homeless. Steve lost a leg to diabetes while he was in prison for some kind of financial fraud. He works at a phone bank now. Dad is, of course, too sick to work. They are each the other's oldest friend. They talked on the phone nearly every day for most of my life. Dad wrote to Steve all the time while he was in prison—long letters about anything and everything, to keep him busy and give him hope. Now that Steve is out, they are in closer proximity to each other than ever before in their lives, and they both have oceans of free time. But they rarely talk on the phone anymore, and they never get together. I don't think that they could bear it.

In the months leading up to his suicide attempt, my father often spoke of feeling "used up," "exhausted," "hopeless," "tired of life." I understood my role as that of the dutiful refuter, arguing that things were different from how he saw them, or at least bound to change. Since his suicide attempt, I no longer argue. Now I hear him out, validate what he's feeling, commiserate to the degree that I am able, and then try to shift the focus of the conversation toward concrete actions we might take to improve his situation. Usually, there are none he will accept. His sisters could come by more often; we could hire someone, maybe; maybe we could afford that. Some version of it. Maybe we could figure out a way. But he doesn't want anyone in his space. He's very firm on this point. And it's true that I cannot imagine him allowing someone—me, my aunts, a stranger—to help him eat, or dress, or use the bathroom. He has never had an ounce of vanity but he has always had a massive, killing pride. Were he to lose his last vestige of self-sufficiency, his martyrdom to his own loneliness, would he even be him anymore? What is he, after all, if not this willful self-destruction? Would ripping back this last veil of his autonomy, flimsy as it is, finally move things forward, force some kind of palliative change, or would it be the ultimate indignity, destroying him once and for all? Or would it not matter? Given that he's going to die, sooner than later, and of this illness, why not let him do it his own way, on his own terms, however deranged those terms may seem from the outside—in other words, to anyone who isn't him?

I don't mean suicide. I mean letting him live his life, whatever's left of it, the way he wants to live it.

Maybe I'm thinking about this in entirely the wrong terms: emotion, will, philosophy, belief. Perhaps I should be thinking in medical-legal language: indigent, disabled, power of attorney. At what point does my presumption of his right to self-determination become itself a form of negligence, of harm?

And who says it will be sooner than later? How could I possibly know that? And when I say "this illness" do I mean Parkinson's or depression? Do I mean poverty? Capitalism? America? He is being killed by the healthcare system at least as much as by bad choices or bad genes. What name will I give his death if he gets one of his dizzy spells and falls down in the shower or on a flight of stairs?

I am never more my father's son than in the way I turn these questions over—point counterpoint subpoint, this way that way, every possible argument arguable—and endlessly. There are no such things as conclusions here. As decisions. When does a willingness to treat a complex issue with the depth and delicacy it warrants descend into Hamlet-like dithering? The form and fact of the question embody the spirit of what it is asking, thus rendering it unanswerable. The question is designed to forestall all action but further consideration of the question. In this way the question is answered: Time decides.

Dad and I can talk for hours. In person or on the phone, our conversations have always been marathons. Two hours is usual; three is not unheard-of. We can talk about anything. He loves to tell old stories, and to hear the minutest details of what's going on in my life. He taught me to be a storyteller, and so I tell him stories: make epic and opera of some student I held after class, some conversation I had with an editor. In one way, these sessions are a kind of charity on my part. I know that all the good news I have to give him about my own career (however tentative or overblown) will carry him for days. But of course I enjoy the attention, the laser-focused love-hot attention; I can never tell him enough about myself and I am the hero of every story that I tell. I come to both crave and resent this dynamic, which I view as unchangeable, though it is of my own invention. It feels like childhood. Thirty, thirty-two, thirty-four years old, answering the equivalent of "What did you do in school today?" for the length of a feature film.

I try to call him once a week, but a week becomes two weeks, three weeks. I tell myself I'm storing up stories for him, which is true, but also I'm exhausted. I'm sick of performing a happiness I don't always feel, and sick of playing his sin-eater. If I take a pause the empty space in the conversation will be filled with his pain and sorrow, which neither of us wants. His depression is always fighting for a way in. A question like "How are you?" can easily open the floodgates, send us down the dark hole of the divorce and his ruined life and ruined body and how tired he is of everything until he is sobbing into the phone telling me how badly he wants to die and he knows he shouldn't be telling me this and he's so sorry to burden me but who else is there to tell, there is no one else, no one else to tell (though of course he's saying all the same things to my sister): *I didn't mean to bring all this up but once I start I don't know how to stop, Justin can you please say something let's just talk about something, say something, change the—*

"I submitted a story to *The Paris Review*."

"What does that mean?"

"Nothing yet. It'll probably come to nothing. But they usually write me back pretty quickly, so I feel like I've got their attention."

"That must be good, right? How many people can say that?"

"Yeah, definitely good, but I mean just by the numbers it's a long shot, so—"

"But you're in the running."

"Yeah."

"So that's great then. And what's *The Paris Review* exactly?

Do they pay well? Is it in French? You don't know French."

"I don't know French."

Lately I'm lucky if I can keep Dad on the phone for an hour. He shakes too much to hold it or to get his headphones on, so he puts it on speaker but he has to keep moving so he can't always stay by where he set it on the table. He paces constantly. Something about movement, using his body, helps mitigate the spasms. Less and less as time goes on, but some. He tells me he's worn a track into the carpet. He basically never sleeps so his mind is always fried—add it to the list of what's been ruined. He doesn't have the focus to read a book or article, probably couldn't sit still long enough to get through it anyway. He repeats himself, his pain litany having long since become repertory. He always has the TV on: CNBC during market hours, MSNBC or CNN after the closing bell, never Fox. But lately he's having a harder time following the news.

As recently as last summer he was lecturing me on the threat of Trump, on Hillary's weakness as a candidate, on the horror awaiting the nation. When Trump's odds were in the single digits all he said was, "Get ready, because it's coming." As I sit here today at the campus Starbucks, under gray Indianapolis skies, I realize that he did not once mention politics when we spoke this morning. The inauguration was two days ago, the Women's March was yesterday (they got six thousand people! in Indianapolis!), and today there are brazen lies spilling out of the White House: Sean Spicer is talking about the size of the crowd in the inauguration photo, Kellyanne Conway just coined the phrase "alternative facts" to the face of a stunned Chuck Todd. This stuff is the bread and butter of his outrage, and a major if bitter vindication: It's all going like he said it would. It's the kind of thing we'd normally fume and crow over together for hours. I am sure it all passed across his TV screen (was on his screen with the volume low but not off even as we were talking) but it only occurs to me now that he didn't bring up any of it. Is it possible he did not understand what he was seeing, or that it registered but quickly passed out of his mind?

I think of *Patrimony*, Philip Roth's memoir of his father Herman's life and grueling final illness. Roth writes of a man who became "utterly isolated within a body that had become a terrifying escape-proof enclosure, the holding pen in a slaughterhouse."

And what it was like, as the son, to watch the walls of that pen close in around his father, to be powerless as he saw and heard and felt his father's terror taking hold.

After Michael bought Dad the apartment—because it was cheaper, in the long run, than renting one for him, to say nothing of what it was costing per week for the hotel room— there arose the issue of reuniting him with his belongings.

This must have been late 2013 or early 2014. At least some of "the Stuff," as he always called it, was really all of ours: family pictures, sets of dishes, my and my sister's childhood things, book collections, school projects, stuffed animals, whatever else. But most of it was his: boxes and boxes of papers from jobs he held decades ago, ancient tax records, his vinyl collection. In the old days he always had the radio on or the turntable going, belting along as the mood struck, at home or in the car or even in public sometimes, singing half under his breath. After he sold the house and moved into the hotel he stopped listening to music, and was perfectly frank about the fact that he would probably never own another record player. (In fact, he did own a record player, along with stereo receiver and speakers. The same rig he'd had since the '70s, kept in mint condition all these years, and it still sounded good as new. It was in the storage unit with the rest of the Stuff.) But he didn't want to listen to the music, had no interest in hearing the grand anthems and love songs of his heyday, all those lyrics he still knew by heart but would no longer sing along with. He had, of course, not so long ago told my sister that the collection was probably worth some money, and suggested she try to sell it. And yet now the idea of parting with the records had become unthinkable to him.

All of the Stuff was in a storage unit in Nashville, and he was in South Florida, and he wanted it all shipped to him. My mother, for her part, was ready to be rid of the storage unit, which she had been paying for, for years. Christ, the way these things have of dragging on, so it feels like time itself has gone gummy, every "issue" a quicksand. Poverty depression indecision. A black hole that neither spits you out nor sucks you in. (By the time this imbroglio resolved itself, the very word "stuff" was effectively soiled; to this day my wife cringes to hear it.)

Dad hadn't wanted to leave the Stuff behind in Nashville in the first place. He was quick to point out that we wouldn't be having this problem now if we'd just listened to him then and brought it with us when we moved him. But this, I reminded him, had been impossible, because at the time the family did not trust him to make the drive alone, and my sister was in law school, so it fell to me to drive with him, and I had been living in New York for so long that I didn't trust myself to drive a U-Haul with a car hitched to it. Plus (I didn't mention this to him) it had taken so long to get him to agree to move back to Florida that we were racing to get it done before he could change his mind. Compared to that problem the idea of the Stuff seemed nebulous and abstract. It was just a bunch of old shit in boxes, right? He hadn't needed it for this long; nobody had needed any of it. We said to each other that once we got him settled in South Florida his sense of imperative would soften, maybe disappear.

This was a lie we told ourselves. We all knew Dad better than that.

I didn't get my driver's license until I was twenty-three. Growing up, I hated driving. I was scared of it. More than that, I hated taking lessons from Dad, who didn't trust Mom to give them and yet was so uptight himself that every lesson devolved into a fight. When I quit he was happy to let me. Mom resented his coddling me on this point; she thought it was infantilizing and the fact was that they could have used the help getting my sister to and from school and extracurriculars, instead of having to ferry the both of us wherever we needed to go. My father defended my decision; he protected me, which I appreciated at the time and still appreciate, at least in principle, though in retrospect I'm not sure that he was right to do so, besides which it's clear now that he was also protecting himself. The truth is that he was scared. As scared as I was and probably even more scared: that I'd hurt myself, that I'd wreck a car he couldn't afford to replace, that I was growing up so fast.

I learned to drive in college, through trial and error (no major errors, thank God) while driving a drunk friend home in her own car or doing my share on a road trip. Bit by bit until I could actually do it. The summer before I started grad school, the learner's permit I had acquired at fifteen years old finally expired. I took the driving test in Tennessee, mostly so I'd have a valid ID in New York City, but over the next decade I never found myself behind the wheel of a car more than once or twice a year.

October 2013: five months after Dad's suicide attempt at the Nashville airport. I flew to Nashville and he picked me up. He'd parked the car in the garage, and there we were walking through it, like this was a regular day and this was a normal place without any deeply upsetting psychic weight attached to it—and who knows, maybe for him it was. He got me my own room at his hotel, using accrued loyalty points, which had been racking up again since May, as we had tried to convince him to come back to South Florida, while scrambling—and failing—to find a place to put him when he got there.

Dad would have stayed at the hotel indefinitely, but in September his mother had fallen and broken her hip. Since George was senile and Barbara was his full-time caretaker, they couldn't live alone while she recovered. They'd been installed at Ronni's apartment in Plantation, Florida. Ronni used her spare bedroom as an office, and was now sleeping on its fold-out couch so that George and Barbara could have the big bed and their own bathroom.

We seized on this development and used it like a battering ram to break down Dad's resistance to relocation, which, insanely, he was still trying to cling to even after everything that had happened. I don't know if he thought Michael would just keep paying for him to live at the Nashville hotel forever, or if he'd planned to ride it out as long as he could and then try to kill himself again. I don't know what he thought. But once we had my grandparents at Ronni's, we were able to insist that Dad take *their* empty apartment while his long-term arrangements were being worked out. We figured—correctly—that if we could just get him down to South Florida he'd stay put, and we got him to agree to come by telling him that Ronni and his parents would need *his* help. As ever, the only way to get him to do something self-preserving was to convince him it was actually in the service of somebody else's need. The only problem with this plan was that it hadn't left us enough time to deal with the Stuff.

Now I was spending the night at the extended-stay hotel that had been my father's pseudo-home for most of the last three years. I wish I could say that the experience was profound or revelatory, but it wasn't. The hotel was anonymous and without character, which is the whole point of hotels like that. It felt like falling asleep inside a piece of clip art. We left Nashville early the next morning, the Nissan packed tight with clothing and a few boxes of I-don't-even-know-what. Whatever he'd deemed too precious to be left behind.

I was supposed to be helping him with the driving but he hardly let me behind the wheel. In those days, the tremors in his arms still went away when there was a task at hand. The engagement of his mind and body overrode whatever was misfiring inside him, and so the network of processes required to operate a car focused and soothed him. Also (he didn't say this, but I knew it) in his mind I was still sixteen years old and didn't know how to drive. The trip was going to be hard enough already without us having to wage a war over that, so I let it pass. He didn't seem to be a danger to himself or the other cars on the road. I did not feel unsafe riding shotgun, fussing with the A/C and the music while he cruised along, the hours chewing through the miles.

_____

Dad always had unfathomable stamina and discipline. When I was three years old, and he was thirty-three, he decided that he needed to get in shape. He got up one day at five-thirty in the morning and went for a run. To his dismay, he could hardly make it through two ten-minute miles. He got up the next day and went again. He kept a log of his daily distances and times. Within a year he was averaging five miles per day at six minutes per mile. To build core strength he did a hundred sit-ups every night, using the living-room couch as a prop for his legs. He did this routine at home and on vacation, seven days a week, no matter what the weather was or how he felt or what else was going on. When he was forced to miss a day, the morning after we were all in a car accident and I was in the ICU, he started his count over again, and after that didn't miss another day for twenty-eight years—that is, until his suicide attempt. A few days later, he started running again, and continued to run, even as his body deteriorated, until he was staggering down the street in Sunrise Lakes, wearing hideous green runners' short-shorts and his "Coach" T-shirt from the years he volunteered at the Special Olympics. By the time he finally gave it up, in the summer of 2016, I was older than he had been when he'd started.

On our road trip we only ever stopped when I got hungry or asked for a bathroom. He hardly seemed to have needs of his own. It's twelve or thirteen hours from Nashville to Plantation. Technically doable in a day but we decided to stop for the night in Gainesville, where he and I and my sister all went to college. This way, we reasoned, we'd arrive around lunchtime the next day instead of in the middle of the night.

We stayed at some place by the highway that took his hotel points. (He would have points for years to come: his single major asset. When I got married—a courthouse wedding, Portland, Oregon, July 20, 2015, he was too sick to travel: Melanie skyped him in, his frail and deeply drawn face bright on the phone screen, sitting in his bedroom, at the desk that I helped him build when he first moved and that he'd later bruise his head on when he fell and got stuck between it and the bed, wearing a shirt and tie that surely dated to his stockbroker days, crying and smiling—he gave us a few nights at a hotel in Seattle for our honeymoon. When we checked in the concierge thanked "Mr. Taylor" for being such a loyal customer, and gave us an upgraded room. We called Dad from the executive suite and thanked him for our gift. We told him it was a hell of a view from up there.)

Dad offered to let me take the car if I wanted to go see the old stomping grounds. Maybe it was me and not him who was hallucinating that I was sixteen again. Maybe, I thought, I don't give him as much credit as he deserves. But I couldn't bring myself to take him up on the offer. I wasn't sure who lived in Gainesville anymore, or—if I did find someone to meet up with—what I'd say when they asked what I was doing in town.

Thanks but no thanks, I told him. He shrugged.

We ate an early-bird dinner at, I think, a Cracker Barrel. We went back to the room, a shared room this time, and watched *Shark Tank*, a reality show about wannabe entrepreneurs. He

59

had very detailed thoughts about the show, about this particular episode (which it turned out he'd seen before), and about entrepreneurship in general. We were asleep by eight o'clock, up the next morning before six. Hotel breakfast and on the road again.

What did Dad and I talk about on our drive? In the hotel room? At breakfast? At dinner? I know we filled the days but so much of the content of what we said has slipped away. He told me about his first days in the brokerage business, how the company that gave him his first job (Bache, I think, though I may be wrong) sent him to New York to train for a few weeks. How he'd never lived in the actual city before, and how there was another new recruit there, a guy from Kentucky, with the heavy accent and everything, who hated the noise and grit and chaos of the place, was terrified of being mugged. How Dad had taken him out on the town—*I had to practically force him to leave the hotel at first, but he got the hang of things eventually*—because he thought it would have been a shame for this guy to go all the way back to Kentucky without having ridden the subway or walked through Chinatown.

He talked a lot about his childhood: his parents' lack of interest in their children, and a sixth-grade teacher who had told him he could do anything, be anything. He remembered her as the first adult who ever gave him strong, unqualified encouragement. Who told him that he had promise, and had seemed to genuinely appreciate him as a person. There had only been a handful of adults in his life who said things like that to him, and she was the first. He still remembered her name and the names of all the other students in that class and what the classroom itself had looked and smelled like. He told me all these things. I wish I had written them down so that I could share them here, so that I could honor that woman's name.

He said he hoped that some of my students might talk about me like that someday.

At one point he told me the story—blow by blow—of an entire season of Little League he coached, a team I must have been on, eight or nine years old, and how he took on the whole Optimist Club over an unfairly umped game, how he knew the whole rule book and lodged a formal protest, demanded and then got a hearing, during the course of which he exposed some kind of self-dealing that had been fucking up the whole league for years (or was the corruption thing related to the peewee basketball league? because I heard that story too) and he was eventually vindicated, though in the course of the crusade he made a lot of enemies. He didn't quite register that last part, but I did, as well as the fact that the men he'd gone up against were mostly other neighborhood dads. People with whom he might have done business, people in whose homes his own children played.

On the last stretch of the second day he finally let me get behind the wheel. It was just enough so that when I told people about my trip I could honestly say I helped my father make the drive to Florida, rather than that I kept him company while he drove me there, though this was in essence what happened. We were getting close to my aunt's apartment. Twenty minutes, fifteen, ten, off the highway now, wending our way through the sunbaked streets of Plantation. The road we were on teed off at a canal. I stopped at the Stop sign, turned to him, and deadpanned: "It's not too late. We could still drive into the canal instead." He laughed harder than I'd heard him laugh in months, if not years. I laughed also, a shared rib-splitting crack-up, the both of us.

In the parking lot at my aunt's development we stood by the car and embraced like we were saying goodbye to each other. He thanked me and said the drive was the best thing that had happened to him in a long, long time. I told him I loved him and he told me he loved me too.

We went inside to face the family.

Depression is a failure of narrative. One effect of trauma is the collapse of the concept of time as distance. Trauma is not just *what happened* but *the fact that* you are no farther from it today than yesterday, or tomorrow. In the night terror of the present tense, foresight becomes a form of déjà vu.

Ronni: "We talked about it when we were older, how bad it was in the house and how we wanted to do better with our own kids. But he never got over it. I used to say to him, 'Whatever it was, it's over now. It's done with. You've got to move on.' But he really couldn't."

When Dad was suicidally depressed we all did whatever we could to convince him there were things to live for. We tried to tell him he was wrong. But that was 2013, and now, four years later, when he speaks about his pain, his exhaustion, the moment-to-moment horror and indignity of his existence—all of which have worsened and are worsening—I sometimes think suicide might be a sane response, a mercy. I never say this to him. But I know he thinks about it, probably constantly. "Every third thought shall be my grave," Prospero says at the end of *The Tempest*. This must be how my father's mind moves. It is how mine moves now, only the grave-thought isn't mine but his, or rather, it is him. His life, his death. It's all pretty much the same to me at this point: illness I cannot cure, pain I cannot know, poverty I can hardly help relieve. The wound—the wound of his suffering, as it has been inflicted on me—will be my scar one day or it is already; or it will never scar, will stay a wound. He is in his apartment right now thinking about doing it, the quickest and surest way, the *tidiest* way. I admit that I'm surprised when he says that he's afraid of the pain. Physical pain never bothered him much, and anyway these days his whole life is pain. When he told me the story of falling by the desk and getting stuck, his fear of starving to death and how long it would take, I barely caught myself, barely cut myself off before offering that I've heard drowning is fairly painless, that there's a canal running along the perimeter of his development, just like the one we joked about driving into. I wonder what it would take to get me to say this to him. I'd like to think that nothing could, but I'm sure that isn't true. I am weak, selfish, angry, and, in my own way, exhausted. I have a hate for him that is hardly distinct from my love. But it would be pointless, this suggestion, because I'm sure he has already thought of it, is thinking of it now, and has held off for his own reasons, whatever they are, and I am trying, trying to be grateful, through all this darkness to be grateful for every hour, every strained conversation, every breakdown, the whole cycle, every awful day he is still here.

To be grateful for that.

Sometimes I wonder if he is asking, in his sidelong way, for permission. That if I were to give some sign of being ready to let him go he'd feel released from the bonds (of fatherhood, of family) that I am sure are the last things keeping him clinging to his wreck of a body, of a life. I imagine myself noble and bold, humane enough to grant this to him. Would he take it? I think maybe yes. And if this is so, then perhaps it is no less than I owe him: this final mercy. A son's understanding. For-giveness and release. If I have what he needs and am capable of giving it, why shouldn't I?

Because it is terrible and wrong, if this is what he is asking. No father should ever ask such a thing of his child. If he wants to die, let him, and let me live with the already considerable trauma of having survived this ordeal. To dare to add to that burden the guilt of permission, of complicity . . . Fuck him for putting me in a place where such a thought is even thinkable. A thousand times fuck him.

How do you save a drowning man who doesn't want a life preserver? Who only seems to want company, a witness, while he sinks as slowly as he can?

But to ask this is to misrepresent his mindset, his intention. If my father could understand that he has become the central trauma of his children's lives he would suffer a heartbreak even deeper than those he's known already. (Milton: *And, in the lowest deep, a lower deep / Still threatening to devour me opens wide . . .*) Countless times I have tried and failed to convince him of the impact that his behavior, his being, has on other people—that we are happy when he is happy, sad when he is sad, et cetera. He understands that his happiness is connected to ours, his children's, but the reciprocal property of the axiom cannot be comprehended. I believe this is because, at a fundamental level, he does not believe he matters to anyone, is incapable of receiving love and so cannot credit the notion that he suffers any way but alone.

"There is no me," he says.

I have heard him say this so many times. It is the howl of the beast that lives at the bottomless bottom of his misery, his sickness, the abomination that feeds on everything that falls down the black well of his suffering. He forces the words out between choking sobs, crying the way a child cries, achieving emptiness. All of this thin and crackling in my earbuds as I pace the apartment (whichever apartment, the years go by) with my phone in my jeans pocket, hot against my thigh.

What should a son say back to that? What would a wife have said? What can anyone say? The statement beggars every possible refutation. The only thing you can do with a ravenous beast that you can't kill and can't catch is try to starve it. So I don't say anything. I take deep breaths and let him hear me breathing, pacing my calm breaths to his ragged ones, until he calms down enough to match me. Until he comes back to himself enough to ask me to change the subject. "What's new with your writing?" he asks, his voice steadying. "What's new at school?"

My aunt Francine once told me that when they were all kids they'd sometimes find him sitting on the stairs looking shell-shocked, crying, saying things like "Nobody loves me" to himself over and over. His siblings didn't know what to make of it, and his parents either did not notice or did not care.

Another way to understand my father, then, is as someone who has lived his whole life as an undiagnosed manic-depressive. At various times various people have suggested that he seek treatment, at least "talk to someone," but he always refused all attempts at intervention and mitigation. I imagine he was scared of what he might learn about himself, and of whether, assuming it worked, he would recognize the version of himself that emerged on the other side. How many of us, after all, can imagine ourselves as wholly separable from our core traumas, our constitutive lacks and faults?

Maybe he never believed that he needed the help.

I doubt that. He was—is—preternaturally intelligent. The most common thing people say about him is that he's one of the smartest people they've ever met. The second most common thing people say about him is that he is intimidating, and can be a real asshole. Even I have to admit that I think of his best and worst qualities as fully interwoven, so that separating them risks eradicating something essential and animating, the thing that makes him him.

I think he always did know what he carried within him, and so it must have been a conscious choice, stubbornness plus fear plus the self-preserving whisper of the sickness, that made him decide to go it alone.

To live his whole life at war with himself.

Why am I writing this?

My motives are largely selfish. The confession and the narrativization are both deeply relieving, even pleasurable. That much must be obvious. It feels good to revel in hot, raw hurt. But there is little that I've said about my father that I don't see some version of in myself. What starts out causal—a new city, a search for work—degrades into causelessness. Suddenly everything is a problem, and it's hard to so much as wash a dish after lunch without cursing the sandwich that got it dirty, the money that the ingredients cost, the dwindling bank account out of which that cost was paid. At a certain point it starts to seem reasonable to leave the dish in the sink, even though that's going to mean an argument later about why you didn't clean up after yourself when you made lunch. And because it will be impossible to explain that the alternative to leaving the dish in the sink was not cleaning the dish, but rather flinging it across the room, you won't give any answer to the question, which will then become a problem in itself.

In 2016, I saw a therapist for the first time. After a few sessions she told me that there was nothing wrong with me, that I was responding appropriately to the objective stress factors in my life: dislocation, unemployment, a sick father, months of rain. I did not need meds, she said, as there was no diagnosis. No cure for the Portland winter or for being part of a family. I wasn't sure she was right, but I wanted to believe her, and so I laughed and she laughed with me. "It's good you don't need medication," she said. "That's a good thing. But without a diagnosis your insurance won't keep covering these visits." Which was too bad because I had found talking about Dad to be extremely cathartic, and pragmatically useful. It forced me to take what I was experiencing and form it into a story that, however halting or inchoate it may have been, at least it had a recognizable shape and features (characters, motives, a plot) as opposed to the amorphous unhappiness that was fucking up my life.

Therapy also kept me from pouring every last drop of my anxiety about Dad onto my wife, in effect reproducing in her the demoralization and exhaustion that talking to him produced in me. The therapist, understanding this, offered to fish a little longer to try to find a diagnosis so that I could keep scheduling sessions, but I told her not to bother. Even with the insurance I was still on the hook for the co-pay, and limited to one visit per month.

My father's whole life may have been ruined by his inability to understand himself as being loved by others. It is likely that this was genetic, hardwired, or, if you prefer the language of spirit (which he wouldn't, but I often do), it is a small black spot on his soul. His parents, through what they did or didn't do, allowed it to spread. Dad has spent the last ten years fighting the decay of his body, but he has been fighting the decay of his soul for far longer; for his whole life. If I believe that, and if I believe that my own soul bears the same black mark, I also believe that it has stayed just that size—a mark, a scar, a tiny blemish—because of what he and my mother did right, the ways they succeeded.

But that it exists at all is a reminder that there is no choice you can make, no parenting strategy you can implement, to fully supersede a genetic predisposition to depression, or the fact that sadness is a part of being human, or that anyone is capable of digging himself into a hole from which he cannot escape without aid.

When my wife texts and says she is missing me while I'm away for so long in Indiana, that she cried yesterday in *savasana* at the end of her yoga class, it is the small stunted dead black part of me that is confused by her words, though I myself felt and feel all those same things. I cried yesterday too. And yet while it makes immediate and complete sense to me that I should love and need and miss her, it is somewhat less self-evident, less reflexively understood, that she should or would feel the same about me. That's the dead spot. But its voice is small and easily silenced. I know it is a liar.

But what if I didn't know that? What if one day I forget?

My father traces his decline to the one-two punch of his marriage collapsing and his illness taking hold. In the version of the story he tells himself, the collapse *causes* the illness, so that all the trauma has its origin in the divorce—an "event" itself years in the making, comprised of countless subsidiary episodes. The marriage was on its last legs before the move to Tennessee, in 2004. The move—which he almost didn't make—was the Hail Mary, the hard reboot, that failed. It's almost as if, having made the move, he thought his work was finished, rather than just beginning. It is possible he believed he had done my mother a great mercy rather than that one had been done by her for him. He wallowed in self-pity, lashed out at the new city, refused to make friends. He made their lives more miserable than I would have thought possible. I wonder now—as I wondered then—what he thought was happening during this period, why it did not occur to him that all these actions would have repercussions, in his marriage or his children's lives or his own life.

Could he really just not see that? Or did he see but not believe?

In 2007 I asked these questions as a son trying to comprehend the behavior of his father. In 2017 I ask them as one married man trying to comprehend another man's marriage. Why it lasted as long as it did and why it failed.

After the divorce was finalized, after he sold the house because he couldn't afford to keep it, after he moved into a hotel because he couldn't bear to leave town, he still wrote his ex-wife letters. Endless emails (I have seen a few), some of which were hateful and recriminatory and implicitly threatening while others were weepy and sentimental and hopeful—even then—of reconciliation.

I have often wondered whether he understood that the sentimental letters were being read by the same person who'd had to read all of the hateful ones. But then, given that the same person wrote both of them, it stands to reason that he was not able to see the disjunction, the nauseating rhetorical swerve from one to the next. The cognitive dissonance he produced was in exact proportion to that which he suffered, and in the end Mom did the only thing she could do: She stopped reading.

My father wanted to design the financial plan for the divorce himself. He didn't trust my mother—by this point the family's sole breadwinner for at least a decade—to manage money. Amazingly, she let him. "He wanted to keep the house," she said, "so he gave me the cash amount he felt was fair. I trusted him completely on this. He wouldn't have lied or cheated—that just wasn't him. The trouble was he wouldn't sell the house, he just sat on it and watched the market decline." This would have been 2008, 2009. Eventually he did sell, at the bottom of the market, and what money he made from the sale was, to put it plainly, pissed away. I don't even know how many thousands of dollars he handed over to the International Hotels Group, getting slowly sicker all the while, until he found himself homeless and suicidal. Now he lives on the charity of his nephew and his ex-wife, on the phone with me and crying himself to the edge of hyperventilation as he tries to explain—again—that he is sorry there's no trust fund, that I have student loan debt, that I have to be absent from my own new marriage for these stints to go where the work is, that after two years in Portland we still can't find a house we can afford. He's sorry that he doesn't have the family house, the one in Florida or the one in Nashville, so that there would be somewhere for everyone to gather. He's sorry that things aren't different. Life wasn't supposed to happen like this. And yet somehow it has.

Fall 2015: The Stuff was still languishing in the storage unit my mother had been paying for. Nobody knew exactly what was in there. Much of it, we suspected, was effectively garbage, not worth what it would cost to ship to Florida, to be crammed into his already cramped apartment. He kept saying he wished there was some way for him to get back to Nashville, to take care of it himself, as he should have done before leaving, *would* have done before leaving, if only we hadn't rushed and rail-roaded him. (Would—we all knew it—*never* have done if he'd been left to his own devices.) But he was no longer well enough to make that drive, much less do the loading and unloading. He had all but stopped eating, was living on a couple bucks' worth of food a day, cereal and juice mostly: a child's diet. His neurologist had told him years ago to eat more red meat, that he needed the B_{12} for dopamine production, but he read somewhere online that protein can interfere with his Levodopa (the anti-shaking medication) and those couple of hours a day when the medicine is working are all he lives for. They're all he talks about. This was one choice he did not hesitate to make.

Mom offered to move everything to the basement of the home she was by this point sharing with her boyfriend. This incensed my father, drove him to resurrect the most horrible things he ever said about her back during their breakup, as well as to recite all the worst things he says she said during that time: that she'd never been happy with him, that she never loved him. That she didn't give a shit about the family photo albums and would just as soon throw them out as keep them.

Did she really say these things? Did she really mean them, and if so, was her earnestness categorical or conditional—that is, tied to the ferocity of the moment?

I have never asked her these questions. Why would I want to know?

And yet here was Dad telling me all these things that I didn't want to know, and didn't know whether to believe. I wasn't sure whether they were more horrendous if they were true or if they were his fantasies—spewing bile for half an hour only to wrap up by reminding me that it is important that I not let this ruin my relationship with my mother, that I must still love her, as indeed he himself still does, and that—again—he is sorry to have told me any of this, only he doesn't have anyone else to talk to so sometimes it all just comes pouring out when he doesn't mean for it to, he's sorry, so, so sorry.

Not sorry enough to not do it, of course, but sorry enough to be sorry that he did.

It occurs to me now that this sounds like gaslighting behavior, predatory and manipulative. I suppose it is, in its way, but it's mostly himself he's playing head games with. I'm just the guy on the other end of the phone call, the witness, the bitter obliging son. His point about the family photo albums, at any rate, was that Mom couldn't be trusted with them. Neither with the childhood keepsakes, boxes of my and my sister's old shit, most of which we'd tried to throw away ourselves many times before but which he kept because he thought we might change our minds one day, and that he would be held to account by us for what was gone.

From his position of utter helplessness he tyrannized us, and because we were hardly two years out from the suicide attempt, we decided—me, my mom, my sister, his sisters, and Michael—to give in. I said that I would go to Nashville, sort through all the Stuff. I'd do it all while I was on the phone with him. I would be his eyes and ears. We'd go through every box, every piece of paper. I promised this to him. He estimated, grudgingly, that we could get the forty boxes down to twenty. Mom found a shipping company willing to take a small order. They had extra room on a truck. I booked my flight. Mom rented a U-Haul van.

There wasn't room to open the boxes at the storage place so we spent the whole first day emptying the unit. Dad couldn't believe it when I told him that everything fit into one van-load. We had a fight on the phone because he insisted that he'd had a 10 × 12 unit and I told him—I was standing in it—that the unit was 5 × 8. He immediately suspected that Mom had downsized without telling him, that half his Stuff was already gone. It took a long time to talk him down: The unit number was the one he'd given me; his directions through the labyrinthine corridors brought me to where he'd said they would. His key turning in his lock, turned by my obedient hand.

When the U-Haul was full, Mom drove it home (it was rented in her name) and I followed in her boyfriend's Tesla, the nicest car I've ever driven or ever expect to drive. She took the highway but I took local roads to buy a little extra alone time. I bluetoothed my phone into the stereo, cranked the volume high. That whole drive was one long moment of feeling supremely my father's son. More than that, I felt like I *was* him, the healthy part of him, the good, sane part, which I knew was still buried inside him somewhere. It was like he was already gone and here was his ghost come back to ride with me over these low green rolling hills. I wouldn't have minded if that drive lasted forever. But then I took the turn onto Mom's street and it was time to park the car, cut the music, get my broke, sick, half-mad father on the phone, and spend the rest of the day trying to get permission to throw away as much of his precious garbage as I possibly could.

That day in 2013 when Dad went missing his death became real to me in a new way. It is right, I think, to say that I began to grieve for him then and that my grieving did not stop when I learned that he was still alive.

The grieving ends two years later, as I sit in a gravel driveway sorting through the Stuff for hours, box by box and page by page, just like I promised. Doing all the things I would do if he had died, and knowing that eventually I'll do it all again, and that when I do I will think about having already done it once before. It is an eerie, almost dissociative feeling: anticipation of a future déjà vu.

I fill so many garbage bags.

Sorting through a box of old documents, most of them destined for the shredder, I find the records of their divorce proceeding. There are stern, terse letters from Mom's attorney demanding various signatures, and Dad's five- and ten-page replies thereto.

I find a poem. A poem? Yes. Handwritten on a legal pad, the same kind of legal pads I favor, a page of lumbering AABB rhymed verse. Addressed to a "you" that is transparently my mother, the poem speaks intensely but opaquely of the speaker's failures, frustrations, and sorrows, as well as the various things for which he holds "you" accountable. It feels wrong to make a copy of this, so I don't, but there are two fragments I will always remember. The first refers to an imminent future time when "I won't be around to spoil your fun." The second refers to "forty-five summers," which is what tips me off that it isn't part of the divorce era at all. My father turned forty-five in 1997; I was fifteen and my sister was nine.

I try to figure out what might have driven him to write a poem, because as far as I know he never wrote another. I can't figure it out. I could ask Mom but I don't. (Hell, I could ask *him* and he'd probably tell me, which is perhaps what I'm most afraid of.) I could also destroy it, whatever it is, and the rest of these papers as well. I could shred them along with the rest of the garbage and play dumb if it comes up later, which it probably won't. But "probably" has proven many times over to be a dangerous word to use with regard to Dad; every time up to now that I've banked on his forgetting about something or letting it go, I have been wrong. That's why I'm sitting in this driveway now. I place the legal pad back in the box where I found it, along with the divorce papers and whatever else might be in there that, if I were to see it, I wouldn't be able to unsee. I tape the box shut, put it with the rest of what we're shipping.

I grieve two years for my father, his life and his death, everything that was said and everything that was left unsaid. I grieve two years for my father and when it is over I lay his ghost to rest, release myself. The long war ends on a warm fall day in Nashville. The only catch is that he is alive when I begin to grieve and he is still alive when I finish, indeed is on the phone with me, live in stereo headphones, ticked off because I've just confessed to having earlier that day thrown away a DVD player that I'd thought he said was broken but which, he now says, works fine and he wanted to keep it. And I would know that, he scolds, if I'd been more careful, if I'd taken the time to test the device, if I'd paid closer attention to the checklist that we've been working from. *All you had to do was listen to me,* he says.

My Back Pages

I moved to New York City (the first time) in 2004, for an internship with *The Nation*. It was a full-time job that paid $150 per week. I came to the city—and, more to the point, to New York media culture—after four years of anarchist squalor in Gainesville, Florida. My admission to this internship program was, to be honest, a fluke. I would never have known such a program existed, or thought to apply to it, if a creative writing professor (and ex–New Yorker) had not suggested it to me. I had come by Jill Ciment's office during my last semester of senior year, basically to ask her what to do with my life. I told her all about how my mother had relocated to Nashville a year ago, and now my father and sister were joining her, and I thought I ought to go there and help them out. I figured, I told her, that I could get hired at a Best Buy, since I'd worked at one throughout high school. "Listen," Jill told me. "You cannot save your family. You need to run away."

As soon as she said it, I knew she was right, but if not for her push toward New York, I'd have probably stayed right where I was. My rent was $300 a month, I was getting by on part-time work at a sandwich shop, and I had plenty of friends in town. It would have been easy (too easy) to spend the next two or three or ten years there.

Jill suggested *The Nation* specifically because she knew I was interested in politics, and because she had an old friend who wrote for them. She offered to write one of the two letters of recommendation that the application required. For the second letter, I turned to my other mentor, Dr. Terry Harpold, an English professor under whose direction I was at that time writing an honors thesis, a Foucauldian reading of H. P. Lovecraft's *At the Mountains of Madness*. (Sure, why not?) In one of the stranger twists of fate my life has ever taken, Dr. Harpold told me that one of the magazine's senior editors was one of his oldest friends. And so, on paper if in no other way (and it really was in no other way), I went from being some nobody from nowhere to being a strong candidate with powerful friends on the inside. I left Gainesville in May 2004, spent the summer in Tennessee, and was in New York by the first of September.

All the other interns in my group were from elite schools in the Northeast, and for most of them this was a second or third internship. They knew each other from Harvard, from Choate, from previous jobs in media. I, on the other hand, had a résumé that—at Dad's insistence—listed the number of words I could type per minute under "skills." The other two pieces of advice Dad gave me: (1) Always take your full lunch hour, and don't work at your desk while you eat. (2) If you're going to go to the East Village, don't go any farther than First Avenue, it simply isn't safe.

Dad, of course, had not spent any significant amount of time in the city since the '60s, and even then he'd been a teenager taking the train in from Long Island. Still, having no other advice to go on, I dutifully followed his, at least until experience proved how obsolete it was. I had never before felt like such a rube as I did those first few months in New York.

I should say here too that none of this would have been possible without my cousin Michael. He was then in his mid-thirties, around the age I am now, working grueling hours as an attorney and living in an apartment just off Times Square. My family could not have bankrolled my excursus into the Narnia of New York media, and I would have needed a second full-time job if I'd had to rent a room. Michael's place was a one-bedroom that couldn't have cracked four hundred square feet, but he bought me an air mattress and pushed the coffee table against the far wall and I lived in his living room, gratis, for four months. Without his generosity, which I now understand he must have done at least in part to pay forward what my father did for him when he was young, I would never have made it to New York.

Working at *The Nation* taught me that having political opinions was not the same thing as having an aptitude for political journalism, or for the clubby culture of the media world. I had, after all, switched my major from journalism to English all of a month into my freshman year of college, and then spent the next four years taking as many creative writing workshops as I could. But if the media world wasn't right for me, it turned out that New York was.

I loved the energy and chaos of it, the fact that you didn't need a car to get anywhere, and that there were always readings to go to: the KGB Bar, Housing Works Bookstore Café, public events at universities, random open mics in cramped basement bars. My favorite part of working at *The Nation* was poring through the shelves of galleys that were always arriving at the office. It blew my mind that there were people who had access to new books months before the rest of the world— and for free! I took as many of those books as I could carry, as often as my bosses would let me take them. I used the stash to pitch and publish my first book reviews, which is ironic to think about now, because the role of a critic is typically to demonstrate authority and render judgment, and the main thing that those books taught me was that I still had a lot to learn.

Two galleys ended up playing small but crucial roles in the path my life took. The first was *Europe Central,* an eight-hundred-page historical novel-in-stories by William T. Vollmann; the other was *Milk,* a strange, spare novella by Darcey Steinke. I'd been a fan of Steinke's since chancing on a copy of her novel *Jesus Saves* at a Borders while in high school (the title far more scandalous, in my Jewish community, than the sex and violence depicted within its pages). Vollmann's baroque maximalism had been a major influence on my undergraduate fiction. I thought of both writers as semi-mythical figures; they might as well have been Kerouac or Rimbaud. But it turned out that they were both real: Vollmann was soon to give a reading at the New School, where it turned out that Darcey Steinke was a professor. I went to the reading and two days later was back on campus for their MFA program's open house, where I learned that they didn't require a GRE (which I wouldn't have had time to take) and that they didn't require my parents to co-sign my loans (which would, again, have been a prohibitive condition). It was the only place I applied.

I hung around the city after the internship ended for as long as I could, but in January 2005, I moved to Portland, Oregon (for the first time), to reunite with some friends from college who had gone out there. In Portland I spent a few more months sleeping in a living room and writing and reading every day. In March, the New School accepted me to their program. I left Portland in May, spent another long summer in Tennessee, and returned to the city to start graduate school in September. I ended up staying for ten years.

I loved every minute of my New York life: the fun parts and the hard parts; every triumph and every setback; every bit of luck and dumb mistake. (I even love my regrets, insofar as one can.) It was in New York that I learned that I could actually have the life I'd always dreamed of having—a writer's life—even as I learned that what that meant, in practical terms, was something far less romantic and far more precarious than I had imagined. Notice, however, that I don't say "than I might have hoped," because the trade-off has always seemed to me like a fair one. Other people have more money, more consistency, more security, more of whatever else people have. Me? I pretty much do what I want all day. I read what I want to read and I think about what I want to think about and I make up whatever I feel like making up, and only after the fact do I stop to wonder whether the world will evince any interest in what I've made. It's a kind of freedom that few people ever know, and fewer still are able to maintain as they get older. (My parents, certainly, never knew anything like it; I'm sure most parents don't.) So it didn't surprise or offend me that such great privilege came at a price, namely, financial security and material comfort.

My parents supported my decisions, even when they didn't understand them, or when they wished I would have chosen a more clearly defined path. For my father, my self-confidence and ambition were a source of particular pride. It made him feel that he had succeeded in doing for me what his own parents had refused to do for him: instilling in your kid the belief that his dreams are worth pursuing. At the same time, it was a source of constant pain for him that he was not in a position to offer financial support. He loved that I was willing to be a struggling artist but hated that I actually had to struggle.

I met Amanda in early September 2010, through a mutual friend. She worked in publishing, but didn't love being stuck in an office (she and a friend of hers often spoke of their "cubicle escape plan") and before long left to become a bookseller. My first book had come out in February, and it had gotten some generous notices, which had in turn opened some doors for me in terms of my nascent academic career. I was making most of my living teaching undergraduate composition at Rutgers–New Brunswick, but now I had a class in the Columbia MFA program as well. My second book was coming out in the new year. (It would be slaughtered by critics, but I didn't know that yet.) It was a time when it felt like anything was possible.

Amanda and I had our first date at a Park Slope bar called Commonwealth. There had been a tornado in Brooklyn earlier that day and I had been worried that she'd cancel. She didn't. I remember walking up to the bar from the Fourth Avenue/Ninth Street subway stop and seeing downed tree limbs. One of those tall vertical BAR signs had been ripped from the building it hung on and was twisted like pipe cleaner, fixed to the brickwork by a single metal thread.

Amanda had arrived first and ordered her own first round. (Her standard first-date practice, she told me later.) We both took our bourbon on the rocks. We talked about books and music. I mentioned that I had tickets to see one of the Pavement reunion shows in Central Park later that month, and she said she didn't really know anything about Pavement but wasn't their lead singer that guy who used to be in the Silver Jews?

Reader, I married her.

The first trip she and I took together was in January 2011, to New Bedford, Massachusetts, to see the annual marathon reading of *Moby-Dick* that takes place at the whaling museum. When she told her mother of the plan, all Lisa could think to say was, "I'm glad you found someone who thinks that's fun." This became the motto of our relationship.

We'd been dating about a year when Amanda's roommate situation broke up, so she moved into my rat-hole four-bedroom apartment in Bushwick, and for three months we lived five people to one bathroom while we looked for our own place. In early 2012 we found a 1.5 bedroom in a thirty-unit building in South Park Slope. The half bedroom was an office just big enough to fit a desk for each of us. A piece of metal sticking out of the wall in the bathroom seemed to be connected to the water heater in some way (it got terrifically hot), and you had to sort of edge around it to use the toilet or the shower, which were themselves so close to each other that you could put your feet in the tub while sitting on the toilet. You could seat four in the "eat-in" kitchen, but only if you stuck the table in the middle of the room, leaving one person blocked in between the stove and counter and the person opposite sitting in the doorway, while the people on each side sat tucked between the table and the wall like bookmarks slipped into books. That apartment was no more than five hundred square feet, but laid out in such a way that, despite everything I just said, it felt bigger. The office and the bedroom were on opposite sides of the place. We were on the third floor and our window faced the interior of the block, so there was no street noise. At just under $1,800 a month, it was a stretch for us but a bargain for the neighborhood. We moved into that apartment just before my thirtieth birthday and I told anyone who'd listen that I expected to turn forty, maybe fifty, still living there.

In February 2013 our one-year lease was up and the owner offered us the option to renew for two years instead of one. We jumped at the chance. A month later, we got a letter informing us of the sale of the building to a Manhattan-based real-estate company, a professional gentrification engine whose formal structure was an inscrutable nest of LLCs.

These vampires immediately set about flipping all the units in the building. Anyone out of lease got a rent hike so steep it sent them packing. Everyone else got buyout offers, the amounts differing based on things like length of tenancy and whether the unit had rent control.

The first few times they called to ask about a buyout, I told them we weren't interested. Weeks went by and the calls kept coming, but their tone changed. Now they were talking about the endless construction they had planned, the rat infestation that would come from that, the plumbing problems they anticipated, and how hard it would be for us to get our heat repaired if, y'know, it just happened to go out in the dead of winter.

Grudgingly, we started talking numbers. Their first offers were criminally low. We had one big thing going for us: the pure luck of being at the start of the twenty-four-month lease. What this meant was that we could afford to play hardball, but we could not wait them out. Every month we lost on our lease made our buyout worth less to them.

By this time Amanda was the director of public programs at a bookstore in SoHo, staging readings, discussions, and other book-related events three or four nights a week, sometimes for crowds of hundreds. She took half days at work and we went apartment hunting, only to find that the market had changed radically in the past year. In 2012, $1,800 had been the top of our range. Now people laughed and hung up on me when I said that. We started naming it as our base.

It was a hot, miserable afternoon, Friday the tenth of May, and we had been out for hours looking at overpriced, awful apartments in neighborhoods we didn't want to live in, driving around with a smarmy Hassidic guy probably five years younger than me, who kept pulling his *hey-from-one-Jew-to-another-this-is-a-good-deal* routine while in actual fact trying to screw us out of a bunch of application fees for places we would never live. I hated him. When it hit four o'clock he told us that he had to get home for Shabbos. Instead of taking us back to where he'd picked us up, which is standard for these things, he got in his car and sped off, leaving us stranded on Court Street in Carroll Gardens. We were hungry, tired, and upset. Amanda wanted to see if we could get hold of someone to take us out to see another place; I was ready to be done for the day. Or maybe it was vice versa; I don't know. What I know is we were on the sidewalk arguing when a woman came tearing out of the storefront that we happened to be standing in front of. She was cursing a blue streak and running to her car to put money in the meter to avoid a ticket. She did not avoid the ticket, and a minute later walked back our way, holding it. "You guys look upset," she said. "Do you need some water?"

She took us into what turned out to be a real-estate office. We drank the cold water she offered and told her our story.

We'd already been booted out of South Slope; even Fort Greene looked like a long shot. There was no going back to Bushwick. We were half-resigned to being pushed out past Bay Ridge, or maybe out of Brooklyn entirely. Carroll Gardens wasn't even a pipe dream: It was a joke. But Nancy, that miracle-worker, said she had a few places to show us, close enough that we could go see them right now if we wanted to.

The Carroll Gardens apartment was maybe seven hundred

square feet, though laid out in a floor-through style so that despite the extra square footage it felt smaller than the Park Slope apartment had. Still, it was perfect for us, and we set about scrambling to get out of our old lease and prepare to make the move.

On May 11, my sister told me that Dad had been in DC visiting her and that he'd gotten choked up when they said goodbye. That wasn't anything special, to be honest. In the last few years he'd become a hair-trigger crier. But, she continued, he had made a point of telling her how proud he was of her and that no matter what happened she couldn't let herself get distracted from achieving what she was working for. It was the "no matter what happens" part that bothered her, and this was why, when the Mother's Day letter was accompanied by a list of passwords and account numbers, she took it—rightly—as a sign of intent, while I interpreted it as more of a "just in case" thing.

Amanda tells me that I was more aware at the time of what was going on than I'm giving myself credit for now. She says that she and I had a few conversations about it, and that while we weren't sure of anything, she had gone so far as to alert her boss that there was a "family situation" and that she might have to travel on short notice. I believe her, but I can only tell this part of the story the way I remember it, the way I told it at the beginning of this book: silence, the throat packed with ice, late-spring sunlight in the home office that would soon no longer be ours. The hot phone in my hand. Me calling and him not answering and me not calling a second time.

We accepted the corporate landlord's buyout offer, told

the broker we were ready to sign the lease on the new place. I remember thinking, *Well, at least there'll be a little money in case Dad needs help*. It was May 12, Mother's Day, and he was trying to kill himself.

What happened in the days that followed? The answer, absurdly and perhaps inevitably, is not much. My aunts, cousins, sister, and I exchanged some phone calls and a lot of emails. We talked about ways we could take better care of Dad, keep a closer eye on things, and be in more regular contact with one another. Noble sentiments were expressed about how it was time for the family to start acting more like a family. For a while, his sisters were calling or emailing him every day, to offer emotional support and obtain proof of life. My sister and I did the same. He moved from the airport hotel back to the extended-stay, with Michael now footing the bill. We raised the prospect of Florida, but he wasn't ready to think about that yet. We deferred to him. Things were getting back to normal. Or what passed for normal with Dad, which in some ways was the most absurd part of the whole episode: that his untenable, ridiculous living situation was now being thought of as some kind of workable status quo. Within a few weeks, the family email chain slowed to a trickle and then dried up entirely. Life went on.

We moved on June first, the busiest moving day in New York City, and in 2013 one of the hottest days of the year. We couldn't find movers at any price, couldn't even rent a U-Haul until the night before, when I used an old trick that Dad had taught me: Call ten minutes before closing and see who'd canceled. He got us a cabin in Yosemite National Park once using this trick, the night before we left Florida for a family vacation when I was nine years old.

Amanda and I rallied a dozen of our friends to help us, working in teams at each apartment. I drove the truck. Now we had a living room that accommodated our still-expanding library, nearly floor-to-ceiling windows in the bedroom, and so much storage that we took the doors off one of the living-room closets and had Amanda's sister (an architect and furniture artisan) install a bar. We moved into that apartment just before I turned thirty-one and I told anyone who'd listen that I expected to turn forty, maybe fifty, still living there.

But life, as usual, had other plans. Amanda had outgrown her job, and after nearly a year of looking in the city had not found anything that made sense as a next move. She decided to apply to be the new manager of a book festival in—of all places—Portland, Oregon. It seemed like a long shot, but one worth taking. I had fond memories of Portland, both from living there in '05 and from visiting friends and giving readings at Powell's when my books came out. I myself had applied for a job at Portland State University earlier that year.

After she was offered the job and accepted it, things began to happen very quickly. I proposed to her over Thanksgiving. This had been on my mind for a while already, and we had talked in general terms about marriage, but the big move and the looming separation while I finished my school year in New York gave me a sense of urgency. We spent Christmas with her parents in Florida and New Year's Eve at home with friends. We flew to Portland on New Year's Day, 2015. I spent two weeks helping her get settled, then came back to New York alone. In addition to my teaching work, we also wanted to hang on to the apartment until she made sure that this new job, this new city, was a keeper. If she wanted to bail, we wanted there to be somewhere for her to come back to. I won't say that I was hoping for this to happen, but I wouldn't have been sorry if it had. Columbia and Pratt had both invited me back for the upcoming school year, and I put off giving them notice for as long as I could.

Those last months in New York were the coldest, loneliest winter I've ever known. I was working on a novel that was going nowhere, drinking too much and too often, endlessly bemoaning the imminent loss of our apartment, my teaching gigs, our friends—*our life*. I would go visit Amanda in Portland and find myself unable to remember all the reasons we'd had for wanting to be there. She would want to explore neighborhoods and I'd drag my feet, thinking all the while of my father, how when he visited Nashville and my mother first tried to show him the house she wanted to buy, he said he didn't want to see it. I worried I was making the same mistakes that he had made, even as I could now see more clearly how and why he had made them. I had crying jags, which had never happened to me before. Amanda wasn't sure I was really going to make the move.

For whatever it's worth, I never considered not joining her, or breaking our engagement, but I can see why she wondered if I would.

Eventually, I told the schools that I was leaving. We started telling people that the apartment would soon be available, and our friends Julie and Gabe ended up taking it. They're a few years younger than us, and it was perfect for them, for what they needed at that time. Movers came on the first of May and because the semester wasn't quite over yet, I moved into a friend's spare room. A week later, I was gone too.

May 12, 2015, was the second anniversary of my father's suicide attempt: unacknowledged, as you might expect. May 15 was his sixty-third birthday. Birthdays were always a hard time of year for Dad. They were also a hard time to be around Dad, because he took the occasion to obsessively rehash his failures—real and imagined—especially the money he had never made, and all of the things he would have done with that money if he had not not made it. The parents of most of the kids I'd grown up with were buying their vacation homes and midlife-crisis Jaguars. Dad didn't crave any of that stuff, though he sometimes accused Mom of having craved it, which I understood to mean that he was sorry he hadn't been able to give it to her.

I called him, of course; a phone call like any other, like the ones we always had: Kill a couple of hours, try to talk about happy things. Amanda and I had sent him a Target gift card, because he wouldn't accept cash from us and there was no present we could have sent him that would have made him happy, but if we sent him a gift card he'd see that the money was already spent and so grudgingly go to the store and use it on clothes, food, medicine—whatever he needed—rather than let it go to waste.

I had a hard time adjusting to Portland. I missed New York: our friends, our apartments, our lives. I didn't like owning a washing machine or driving a car. I felt isolated, physically and emotionally; both stranded and adrift. I was hardly writing, and what I was producing was no good. I didn't know when I would have a job again or what that job would be. Here we were: new city, new marriage, new everything, and all I felt was that I was failing, had perhaps already failed.

A lot of people put a lot of energy into making me feel welcome, but it was like they were all shouting and waving through smoked glass. Because I'd never experienced depression before, I didn't know what it would look or feel like, apart from what I'd read about it. Here's William Styron, from *Darkness Visible*, which I'd read shortly after my father's suicide attempt, to try to glean some insight into things that he might have experienced but couldn't or wouldn't say himself.

> I was feeling in my mind a sensation close to, but indescribably different from, actual pain. This leads me to touch again on the elusive nature of such distress. That the word "indescribable" should present itself is not fortuitous, since it has to be emphasized that if the pain

were readily describable most of the countless sufferers from this ancient affliction would have been able to confidently depict for their friends and loved ones (even their physicians) some of the actual dimensions of their torment, and perhaps elicit a comprehension that has been generally lacking; such incomprehension has usually been due not to a failure of sympathy but to the basic inability of healthy people to imagine a form of torment so alien to everyday experience.

The title, *Darkness Visible*, is from *Paradise Lost*. It is Milton's description of Hell:

No light; but rather darkness visible
Served only to discover sights of woe,
Regions of sorrow, doleful shades, where peace
And rest can never dwell, hope never comes
That comes to all, but torture without end
Still urges, and a fiery deluge, fed
With ever-burning sulphur unconsumed.

Styron's account rings true to me, in kind if not degree. I spent a lot of time wrapped in what felt like a blanket of gray noise, which made it difficult to navigate basic emotional exchanges, or to communicate what I was feeling to the people around me, or even to myself. I was for the first time experiencing some version of what my father had been struggling with for years by now: dislocation, unemployment, dimming prospects, a sense (right or wrong) of profound worthlessness.

I feared I was becoming more and more like him, even as I was coming to understand what he had gone through, and was still going through, more deeply than I had before.

I felt, and to some extent still feel, deep shame about my failure to understand him sooner or better or more fully than I was able to. *All you had to do was listen to me.* I sometimes think that even though we were never estranged from each other, and even though there was never a time that I would have characterized our relationship as anything other than close and loving, there is no disputing the fact that after the letter I wrote to him in 2007, probably because of it, that relationship began to fracture.

I was disappointed in his decision to stay in Tennessee after the divorce, and frustrated by his refusal or inability to find a job. By this point he hadn't worked in nearly ten years. I don't know what he might have done, since he didn't have a broker-age license anymore and was starting to get sicker—the Parkin-son's appearing as little more than a nervous tic, but no longer something you had to look for in order to notice. It was impos-sible to distinguish between the real limits on his options and his tendency toward self-destruction (if that's not saying the same thing twice). To avoid the tense and complicated dance of dividing my time between him and Mom on visits to Nashville, I stopped going there. My sister was out of school by then: She worked in South Florida for a year, then moved to DC for law school. Mom came to New York a few times a year, for business as well as to visit. I invited Dad to visit (he wouldn't come) and told myself I'd visit him when he moved back to Florida, which I was still trying to convince myself might happen sooner rather than later. Instead, he hung onto the house as long as he could and then dug in his heels at the extended-stay hotel. Years went by without us seeing each other.

There was one visit to Nashville in 2011, a three-day weekend where we rendezvoused with Amanda's parents and sister. We got everyone together on Friday for lunch and a trip to the art museum. On Saturday, he and I went to dinner with Amanda's family. He was affable, maybe a little quiet. I could tell he was trying to be on his best behavior, and also that he was having trouble maintaining a veneer of normalcy—holding his utensils was a struggle, but my offer to cut up his food for him was dismissed. At that point it had probably been years since he'd been to a nice restaurant or socialized with new people. By the end of the night I could tell how worn out he was.

On Sunday, we spent the morning just with Mom before flying back to New York. A few days later, he wrote me a long angry letter in which he argued that it had been wrong to divide up the time so evenly, since Mom saw me so much more often than he did (he was probably right about that) and went on to accuse me of having "taken her side" in the divorce and, more generally, of having chosen her over him. The latter charges were well over the line and I let him know it. After that, whenever he tried to raise the subject of the divorce, I tended to shut the conversation down, which I think is why he began to feel that he couldn't fully rely on or trust me, though judging from his letter it's arguable that he had already been feeling that way for some time.

It is likely that our fractured relationship, and my failure to recognize that fracture as such, left him feeling more isolated and like he had failed as a father, and so became a compounding element of his despair, a contributing factor to his decision to end his life.

And yet my writer-self knows better than to trust such tidy framing. In insisting on the primacy of these grave filial failures (whether real or imagined) and in choosing my own action as the inciting incident, I place myself at the center of my father's story. I displace my mother, my sister, his family, his history: I displace *him*. Of course we're talking about a person who had no sense of primacy in his own life, who did not believe himself entitled to be the center of anyone's attention, which is why he rarely ever claimed it except by accident—when repressed ego would mutiny into id-driven rage. At some level, then, by shifting the focus from him to myself, I'm only doing what he would have done, though I'm not sure that makes it justifiable.

But I had troubles of my own, and Dad had obligations—to me as his son, to our relationship as a relationship, to himself as a man—that he failed to fulfill. Moreover, it is too easy (I mean in a narrative sense) to fault myself for failing to become his caregiver at a time before I was financially or emotionally capable of providing any degree of care. If all the same things that happened to him while my sister and I were in our twenties had happened ten years later—that is, now—we would have reacted much faster and had far more resources on which to draw. But if we're going to play that game then we can say that if all the same things had happened ten years earlier, during our childhoods, who knows how badly it might have fucked us up and where we'd be—or who we'd be—today?

So is this the story of a son failing a father or is it the story of a father failing a son? It's both, I think, which to me is the same as saying that it's neither.

A Brief Aside

A manda and I do not plan to have children. The reasons for this are, as with any couple, complicated. Or maybe they aren't. There are thousands of books and articles that you can read about the pros, cons, and what-ifs of procreation, so I'm not going to dwell on them here. The bottom line for us is that it's not something we see fitting into our lives. And yet, despite our being in agreement on this, I have always had a difficult time saying it—to her, to our families, to our friends, to myself. It's surprising, frankly, that I have managed to make myself write this paragraph and put it here for you to read.

My mother would very much like grandchildren. She has been un-shy about saying so, but knows that in the end it isn't her decision to make, as the children would not be her responsibility to raise. She regards having children as the single most rewarding experience of her life, and it makes her sad to think that I might not get to have that experience myself. To be honest, it makes me sad also, to think about missing out on all that, but not *so* sad that I'm willing to do the things that I would need to do in order to make it happen.

For one thing, I would probably need to get a different wife, and I don't want a different wife. If Amanda is 80-20 against having kids, let's say that I'm 70-30 against. I can get as close as 60-40 if you let me hold a baby for a while, but the odds never break even, much less tip into the procreative side of the scale. Like a lot of men raised with all the privileges of patriarchy, for most of my life I carried an unacknowledged and unchallenged assumption that ambivalence about kids was my birthright. I could stay on the fence about it, and eventually some woman would come along and make me do it, and I would do it, maybe less grudgingly than I was letting on (or maybe not), and then I'd either be a good dad or a bad one, and when it was going well I would tell people laughingly about how I had been hesitant but she made me and it was the best thing we ever did; and when it was going poorly I would convince myself that I only did it because she insisted, curse her for costing me my freedom and my life's work.

This is an extreme description, admittedly a bit cartoonish, but I don't think it's that far off from what a lot of men of my generation go through, perhaps what most men in most generations go through. (Notably, this is not an ideology my own father exhibited. For all his hesitation to have children, for all his fear about love and money and safety, he shared my mother's view that parenthood was the most rewarding experience he ever had.) What this performative ambivalence says, though you never quite actually say it (which is a privilege in itself) is that someone else is going to have to do the hard work for you, to bear, in turn, the burdens of desire, conviction, and consequence, while the nominal "partner" plays Hamlet, or maybe just plays video games. Because I decided to share my life with a woman who was not interested in assuming the role of beleaguered persuader, and who was bracingly forthright about what she did and did not want for herself, I was forced to reckon with what I actually wanted for myself, and by extension for us.

So what do I want? I want the life I have more than the life I might have had instead. I want to not make the compromises my parents made. I want to not struggle the way they struggled or live a life that looks like theirs. I have different priorities, and different struggles, and so will set different goals than they did, make different compromises than they made, succeed or fail on entirely different terms. For them, there were a lot of things they were willing to give up in order to have children. For me, having children is the thing I'm willing to give up.

I like kids. I think they're fun. I don't mind changing diapers, playing games with toddlers, chatting with teens. I like being a cousin, a family friend; I'd make a good godfather, I think. I have a strong bond with our cat. Does it follow, therefore, that I would be able to stay calm when I got the phone call from the school about the broken arm? When the late-night text buzzed, "Dad I'm at this party and I need you to pick me up . . ."

Would I scream myself hoarse like my father used to when the bad grade appeared on the report card? Would I walk away from my writing career, the hard-fought-for, jealously protected, hardly lucrative, and absolutely not child-sustaining passion around which I have organized my entire life? If making that sacrifice is what it took to put food on the table? If it ensured that Junior got to go to summer camp? Can I imagine that child one day writing me a letter like the one I wrote to my own father? Can I imagine myself reading that letter, and what it would say? What are the great charges that would be levied against me, and would I plead guilty or not guilty? What would I write back by way of explanation, apology, or defense?

The answer to some or all of the questions posed above might well be quite compelling (or elating or terrifying), but I've obviated the need to ask them. There is no right or wrong here, no good choice or bad choice—only the choice we made, and continue to make. It does not bother me that I'm not going to be somebody's father. But it does raise a practical question: What to do with all these broadly dadlike instincts, with the urge to be, if not a father, at least *fatherly*?

In a host of obvious and not-so-obvious ways, teacher-student relationships are familial, pseudo-parental. I didn't think about this when I was on the student side of that binary, but after we left New York, I found myself thinking about it all the time, and lamenting what I'd lost. If you've ever tried to earn a living as an adjunct professor, you know how absurd this sounds. I was free of the adjunct hamster wheel, free of New

York rent, *free to write*. But it turned out that I'd invested a lot more than I'd realized in my identity as a teacher.

To be really, really clear here: My students are not my children. First of all, they are adults, eighteen at the very youngest, and some of them much older. (Some are older than I am.) Second of all, they already have parents. But for an aspiring artist of any kind, and maybe for a writer especially, unless you are yourself the child of a successful artist (which comes with its own set of challenges), it is all but guaranteed that your parents won't understand your artistic ambition, and may not condone it. Even if they want to, they probably won't know how. I can barely imagine what my parents must have made of my elementary school attempts to emulate the Stephen King books they probably should have known better than to let me read, or my attempts at "transgressive" fiction and "experimental" poetry during college. Forget the mortification induced by the subject matter or the neophyte execution; they had no contextual framework for (or interest in) the forms themselves.

For the average kid who grows up aspiring to write, and who for that reason enrolls in a creative writing class when she gets to college, the professor she encounters in that classroom is probably the first person she has ever met who has written a book, much less published one. And when you're teaching freshmen, as I did at the Pratt Institute, it is furthermore likely that you are the first adult to consider that student's work seriously or at any significant length. You're likely the first person in her life to read the work *as* work, to call it by that name. You're also the first adult to spend consistent, significant amounts of time around these kids during their first months and years out of their parents' house. They do a lot of growing up in front of you, both on the page and in the classroom and at bars a few blocks off-campus where you weren't expecting to run into them and vice versa. They will date one another and submit their breakup dramas to the workshop as fiction. They will, in one memorable case, show up to class without pants on—because, they'll explain, they couldn't find any pants in their dorm room but they didn't want to miss class. (You will not ask them why their room had no pants in it.) You will assign them Maggie Nelson's *The Argonauts* and they will use their critical response paper to come out to you (and possibly to themselves) as gender-queer.

Only a fool would deny that there is something parental about all of this. For some teachers, that's the worst part of the job. They'll do what they can to keep boundaries firm, and themselves aloof, and I'll allow that there is a lesson worth learning from that kind of teacher: A person who won't help you clean up your mess teaches you how to clean it up on your own, or at least how to leave it at the classroom door. Personally, I don't mind some mess.

Boundaries, of course, are important. Some should never be crossed. I think we all know (or ought to know) what those are. The creative arts are necessarily intimate disciplines. People trust you with their vulnerability, their ambition, their talent, and their dreams. We need not rehearse here the ways that such trust can be abused or exploited. But it seems to me cruel and counterproductive to ignore or stifle all possible intimacy rather than to honor and make use of it. The model is filial, not erotic.

A classroom on the first day of the semester is a gathering of strangers: Some of these people you'll come to know and grow to care for; others you'll hardly be able to stand. Some of your early predictions about who falls into which category will prove mistaken. Some will sit at the back and stay quiet, turn in their adequate work on time, and you'll never get to know them at all. But every student deserves the chance to make the profound connection, to have their breakthrough, for this class to be the best class they ever took. The teacher's job is to make the space of the classroom as productive and inclusive as possible. If you do that, if you give as much as you are able, then it's up to each student to take what they need and leave the rest. It may be that the single most important thing you have to offer them is one possible model for one way of living: not a *should* but a *could*. You're confirming for them something that they've always suspected or hoped was true, but had never before been able to prove. Namely, that people like you exist and that a life like yours is possible.

In my first years as a teacher, my primary concern was to eke out a living while protecting my time so I could write. As I got more used to doing the work (and after I had put a couple of books into the world) I came to understand teaching as a vocation in itself. I began to think more about the role I was playing in my students' lives, and what it would take to try to be for them what my own best teachers had been for me.

Spending time with precocious, dedicated, aspiring writers has been a major boon to my own creative and intellectual life. Being there for students and helping them succeed is a source of personal as well as professional validation. I enjoy teaching, feel nourished by it in what I imagine is much the same way my father felt teaching his nephews to throw a baseball back before I was born, or coaching my Little League teams, which he did for every team I ever played on and then kept doing for years after I quit. He spent countless hours with other fathers' sons, teaching them what their own fathers couldn't and what his own son didn't want to know. I know that I am lucky to have had him as a role model, and that the depth of his attention and the democracy of his approach are foundational elements of my own pedagogy.

It feels good to be good at something, to share what you know, to have people remember you as the person who took the time, who changed their life for the better in however great or small a way. It wasn't until I experienced the radical isolation and dislocation that followed my departure from New York that I realized the full extent of what teaching had been doing for me, which is one reason why, when the opportunity to teach again presented itself, I jumped at the chance. Even though it meant stepping back into dislocation, even though it would ultimately mean nearly two years alone on the road.

Riding with the Ghost

Every time I drove to the Kroger out on Keystone Avenue, past an ugly strip of vape stores and fast-food joints, I noticed a billboard for the Indy Arms Company, a gun shop and shooting range. The winter was bleak, the cold gray days bleeding together. Dad was a mess: physically weak, an emotional wreck, his anti-shaking medication increasingly unreliable in its efficacy. On dragged the weeks and then months after the inauguration. On social media and cable news people were working themselves into fits about how Trump was about to resign in disgrace and flee to Russia, or the "Deep State" was going to sabotage the will of the people by undermining him, or maybe they were going to save us from the autocratic coup he was planning, or maybe had already carried out.

I was halfway through my time in Indianapolis as Butler's writer-in-residence. I was looking forward to getting back to

Portland, but I knew that I would find myself in the same situation I'd been in before I left: lonely, unemployed, adrift in both my daily life and my larger sense of myself as a writer. One of my self-imposed goals for Indianapolis was to finish the novel that I'd started in 2014 and had been in an on-off relationship with ever since. Now there were no more excuses. I had the time, the space, and the job title. All that was left was for me to do the work. But the work wasn't working, and the deeper I dug into the project, the more certain I became that it never would. The book wasn't good, it wasn't going to get better, and I didn't want to spend any more of my life in its claustrophobic, half-baked world. There was some relief, even liberation, in admitting this to myself, but that small comfort was far outmatched by a feeling of loss: for my wasted time and energy, for the hopes I'd harbored for the novel (the usual: fortune, acclaim, et cetera). My job title felt fraudulent; my career like it was over. And there was that sign on the road again, the huge crosshairs logo, and me with my little tote bag full of chicken breast and organic bell peppers, taking a long look as I drove past.

Other than .22s at summer camp, the only time I had ever fired guns was during college, at an anarcho-communist pecan farm outside of Gainesville, Florida, during the Christmas break of my freshman year. I spent two weeks out there helping plant a thousand pine saplings in one of their fields. The plan was to grow the pines, harvest the timber, and use the money to pay off the mortgage and thus ensure the farm to anarcho-communism for all time. I loved these people and was eager to live in their dream, if only for the break between semesters. On New Year's Day 2001 we shot up stacks of old TVs that they had been saving for the occasion. I remember a revolver, and a shotgun loaded with what somebody called "pumpkin balls." I remember the level and aim and the indrawn breath and the trigger pull, how it takes more force than you think it would ("eight pounds," they say, which isn't much for an arm but is substantial for an index finger) and the faces of those TVs as they sagged and spidered. The power that you felt knowing that you had flung that damage across the distance, the stacks wobbling and eventually toppling over. And the way that we talked, calm and casual, about how after the revolution came these were the kinds of skills we were going to want to have.

Was all that really sixteen years ago and longer? And now, perhaps, a revolution had come, only not the one we'd banked on. Indiana has long been a hotbed for white supremacy, and there was a lot of fear in the air—on the Internet, on the news, in nervous chitchat—that violence might break out at any time. Also, my in-laws are gun owners. (Responsible ones, it should be said.) They both grew up in the Deep South and have concealed-carry permits. Once I was out on my father-in-law's boat, just me and him, and he asked me to get him something from the glove box because he was steering. In reaching for it I passed my hand over a pistol, which in my innocence I thought must be a flare gun, and when I said something to that effect he let out a short laugh and gave me a look I hope to never again see on his face so long as I am married to his daughter.

I had thought at various times about asking him to take me shooting; I thought we might both enjoy that. But I had never asked, in part because I hadn't wanted to admit that if we did go, he would have to teach me how to shoot. (Could it go without saying that we were out on his boat that day because he was patiently teaching me to fish?) Here then was another factor in my abiding interest in the Indy Arms Company.

At the same time, I knew, I was doing this at least in part to be able to tell the story of having done it, a story I could tell Dad, or whoever else—the story of that time I went and shot guns in Indiana. But I didn't tell anyone. Why not? Because I couldn't explain what I was drawn by. Because I wanted to live alone with the idea—which included not just shooting a gun but also, perhaps, buying one—a bit longer. Because I knew he would try to give me advice, teach me over the phone everything he knew (or thought he knew) about marksmanship, all of which would be based on forty-year-old knowledge, itself gleaned from a different kind of gun entirely, an ancient rifle from a stint on his high school shooting team, an episode he'd never mentioned until the day I found the weapon—still in its original case, with two boxes of bullets—amid the Stuff in the Nashville storage unit. Against my better judgment, I'd shipped it to him with everything else, and so it sat now in his bedroom closet at the Sunrise Lakes apartment. I did not want to get him talking about that gun.

I went to the range on March 22 at 10 A.M. for their Introduction to Handguns class, which got me the instruction I needed, a gun to use, range time, and a dozen bullets—all for one tidy package price. It turned out that I was the only person who'd signed up for the session, and so the "class" became a private lesson. The instructor was a local kid, twenty-five or twenty-six, an Afghan war vet, honorably discharged after an injury that may or may not have been suffered on the field of battle but was in any case not visible. Something about his back, I think he said. I thought about the experiential and psychic gulf between what he was doing at twenty-three and what I was doing at that same age, between his life and mine.

I marched against the wars he fought in back when he was still too young to fight in them. We had tried to stop them before they started but the wars came anyway and they never ended so he came of age and went to fight, and they were still being fought without him now as he sat in a windowless classroom tucked between the storefront and the firing range, teaching an erstwhile Jew from Miami the right way to hold and load a Sig Sauer P226, the standard-issue infantry sidearm, same as he had carried in the desert.

It wasn't a real Sig Sauer I was holding. Not yet. This was a dummy gun. He was teaching me how to load a clip and work the safety, the correct overlay of fingers in the two-handed grip. He taught me a breathing exercise that I recognized from yoga. I did not tell him this.

When he deemed me ready for the real gun, we went out to the range. He had warned me about the kickback on the Sig, which is an automatic pistol, but I didn't understand what he was saying until I squeezed off the first round. The gun bucked like a mule and I found myself pointing its lightly smoking barrel at the ceiling, the spent shell having spit itself back at me, bounced off my glasses, and fallen into the collar of my shirt. My teacher took all this in stride.

Slowly I got steadier, less skittish. I put some holes in the orange silhouette on the target.

I asked if I could switch to another gun. He said the AR-15 was a lot of fun but I didn't want to spend that much money on bullets, so I asked for a .357 magnum (the only other gun I knew the name of), which was heavier than the Sig, but for that reason easier to hold steady. Without the automatic's fierce recoil to reckon with I did a better job of maintaining my aim. A half dozen holes appeared in the target. And sure they were low and to the right, hardly kill shots, but there they were within a couple of inches of each other, clustered like a constellation in the belly of the silhouette.

The whole experience lasted two hours and cost me a hundred bucks. I remember I thought that I should tip him but I'm not sure if I did, or if I did whether he accepted. I knew that I would not be returning to this place. My purpose in coming here had been to attach experience, something known and felt, to the otherwise largely abstract concept of "a gun." (Abstract to me, I mean.) Now I knew something specific and untranslatable: the weight and heat of metal; the river of silence that ran between the click of the magnum's hammer pulling back and the thunder of its falling forward.

As he rang me up at the front register, my teacher suggested I consider getting a range membership. I told him I was in town for work (I couldn't bring myself to say the word "semester," much less "writer-in-residence") and that I only had a month to go before I left. "Well, heck," he said, "if you're only here a little bit, one thing you've *got* to do is see the tiger sanctuary."

"The tiger sanctuary?" I said.

"The tiger sanctuary," he said. "Out in Center Point."

An old man, a grizzled type, the kind of guy with whom I had expected to spend a morning such as this one, emerged from the back room of the shop. "Y'all talking about the tiger sanctuary?" he said.

"Yeah," I said. "You been out there too?"

"Best ten dollars you will spend in this life," he said. "And it's not just tigers neither."

The tiger sanctuary is an hour and twenty minutes due west of Indianapolis. I drove out on Wednesday the twenty-ninth of March, late enough in the morning to miss rush-hour traffic but not so late that I'd have to hurry to make it back for my evening class. I was in the mood to drive and play loud music and be alone with my thoughts. One week—to the day and almost to the hour—since my visit to the shooting range. I had already begun to polish and revise the scene at the cash register with the two men—that is, the scene you just read— though at this point I had no notion of you who are reading this, or indeed of this book you are reading: I was "writing" it as a story that I'd tell Dad. We'd last talked a week and a half earlier, so we were due for another call.

The guys at the gun shop had described the sanctuary as

a place of profundity and desolation. (They didn't actually say those things, but I got the sense that that was what they meant.) On the day they'd visited they'd been the only people out there and so had enjoyed a tour no less intimate than the private shooting lesson I'd lucked into. Their guide had even let them touch the flank of one of the tigers, and it was on account of this transformative encounter with the very breathing muscle of wild nature that the old man had deemed the admission fee to be the ten best-spent dollars of his life.

I cued up Songs: Ohia's album *The Magnolia Electric Co.* and hit the highway. *Magnolia* is a strange and beautiful album, an all-time favorite. Jason Molina, the songwriter and bandleader, had a style at once forlorn and anthemic. His work is haunted and haunting. He was from that part of the country where the South and the Midwest mingle like brackish water—Ohio, West Virginia—where Chicago is the city people dream of, not New York. The record label that broke him big (as big as he got) is based in Bloomington, Indiana. It felt special to listen to this music, that spirit and that voice, in the region where much of it had been written and performed, and with which it was always concerned.

Jason Molina was an alcoholic. This was not widely known until after he died, in March 2013, succumbing to complications from an illness instigated by his disease. He was thirty-nine years old. I had interviewed him once, in 2010. A fan, I'd emailed him out of the blue and asked for a phone call, which he generously gave to me. *Josephine,* which would prove to be Molina's last LP, had come out about a year before. The band was on hiatus and he was living in England, where he'd moved for his wife's job. He alluded a few times in our talk to health issues, a chronic illness, but did not specify what it was. At one point I asked him outright and he said he didn't want to say. I thought maybe he'd had cancer. I realize now that he meant addiction, and almost certainly depression too. There are references to illness, to the degradation and soul damage that come with permanent sickness, threaded all throughout his vast body of work. Molina made the most he could of a suffering that ultimately proved beyond endurance. He packed a whole life's work into the too-short time he had.

We talked for hours. I asked him dense, writerly questions about his lyrics, and he gamely answered all of them. I think he was surprised and pleased to learn that there was someone out there reading his stuff closely, as though it were poetry. I wanted to know about the way he composed, why he came back to certain images or ideas over and over again, and what it all meant to him.

"I think of a song as something you build," he told me.

It's not something that you do, it's not something that comes out of your gut. It's like you have bricks, you have mortar, you have a trowel—You don't have a building plan yet, you just have all the raw materials and you just start building it and you hope to god you get something good. But as far as the imagery goes, I've always treated it as a rebus. These images all fit into a storyline that is completely open to the interpretation of anybody who listens to it. If you sit down and look at all the lyrics to all the songs, you'll see that there is a theme, but it's not running in a straight line. It's like the dawn coming on, or dusk. It's always in that purple-grey area. But when I say a mule, I really mean a mule, and when I say the horizon I really mean the horizon.

Later in the conversation I asked him about ghosts. "Ghost" is a crucial word for Molina. It may be his most consistent recurring image. For that reason, among others, I wanted to know whether the ghost was as real to him as the horizon and the mule. He said yes without hesitation.

Seven years after that conversation, Molina was dead and I was living in the part of the country that had made and shaped him, driving a road (I-70 West) that he had surely known well. Moreover, I knew some things about loneliness, about illness and dislocation, that I had not known in 2010. And I had far more yet to learn about all of these, but for the time being I knew enough to sense the scope and depth of what Molina had meant when he wrote a song whose first line was its name and the line was "I've been riding with the ghost." He was the ghost I rode with that day, but he wasn't the only one.

As I drove west on I-70 with *Magnolia Electric Co.* blasting, my thoughts drifted from Jason Molina, from Indiana, and back toward New York, where, a few months earlier, my friend and former student Eli Todd had overdosed on heroin and died. He was twenty-three years old. Eli had been my student at the Pratt Institute. I'd begun teaching there in 2011, the same year he'd started as a freshman, and I became close not just with him but with several students in that year's cohort. They were a great bunch of kids: smart, excitable, unruly, up for any academic or creative challenge I threw their way. As things turned out, my four years as a teacher at Pratt coincided exactly with theirs as students. I kept in touch with a number of them after we went our separate ways. Eli and I traded jokes on Twitter; we emailed about music. I asked to see his work sometimes, and we met up when I visited New York. He was among the most promising young writers I've ever worked with, and though still very much finding his voice, had at twenty-one and twenty-two years old already produced a few stories that I thought worthy of publication.

I took one for a small DIY arts journal that I ran with a friend of mine. I took another for *The Literary Review,* where I was the fiction editor. *TLR* hosted an issue-release party at a bookstore in Brooklyn in May 2016. I came back to the city for it and Eli was one of the readers. I took him and another old student, Gabe, to the after-party.

At some point in the night, both of us deep in our cups, Eli told me a garbled story about having gone through a period where he was messing around with pills. Opiates, specifically. He kept the details vague. The only thing he told me clearly, and emphatically, was that it was all in the past. There were no lingering issues and he wasn't an addict. It was just this weird thing he'd struggled with but had gotten over, nothing to worry about, he didn't even know why he was telling me.

Of course, I did worry. It was alarming to hear these things, and the fact that he had confessed them non sequitur suggested that the issue wasn't as firmly settled as he thought it was, or rather, as he wanted me to think that it was. Or he knew that it wasn't and that was why he'd broached the subject. He didn't say anything about heroin, which would have immediately changed the whole tenor of the conversation, which he would have been aware of, which I assume is why he didn't say it. He wasn't a junkie, but he had a junkie's instinct for knowing how to play his audience, how to turn even a tell-all confession into a sort of performance. Perversely yet unsurprisingly, this natural affinity for narrative was what made him such a talented fiction writer.

I will never know if there was something else I could have done or said in that moment that might have changed things for him; I'd like to believe there wasn't, but I also know better than to trust such a self-exculpatory thought. For what it's worth, I gave him a lecture. I told him I was sorry to treat him like a student again, but that since he'd brought it up he should know just how stupid a thing he'd done, that it wasn't worth the risk. I said all the things that you're supposed to say, though I honestly wasn't thinking in terms of mortal danger so much as the drag of rehab, the rounds of kicking and relapse, the needless delay on the road to the real life it seemed so obvious that he had waiting for him. I told him to call me if he ever felt like he was falling off the wagon. He told me again that it was all in the past, and not to sweat it; I told him to just remember what I'd said. He promised that he would. And then, because there was nothing else to be said, we changed the subject. We left the party soon afterward, said good night. I hugged him, hugged Gabe. It was the last time I saw Eli alive.

We were in touch throughout the summer and fall. The last time we spoke was October 18, 2016, on Twitter. He tweeted "well the time has come and im getting rly into the dead again guys." By this he meant the Grateful Dead, a sort of open-secret guilty pleasure of his, and one of the things we shared. Gabe, who after graduation had gone home to New Mexico, replied to Eli with a link to a Phish show and the comment "i don't know if you've ever heard of this band but i think you'd like them." I was sitting in my home office in Portland when I saw this, and I laughed out loud.

To understand why this is funny, you'd have to know that Deadheads tend to think of ourselves as categorically separate from fans of jam bands in general. In fact, Eli had a long-standing conviction that the Dead "weren't really a jam band" at all, because their radical approach was without precedent at the time that they took it; that is, the Dead worked without the model of the Dead, which all subsequent jam bands have had to draw on. This is ridiculous, of course—I mean, it's utterly absurd—and yet I find that I agree with it completely. If anything, I'm jealous that I never thought to make this argument myself.

I sent Eli a YouTube link to the Dead show that had

been preoccupying me of late: July 8, 1978, the second night of a two-night stand at Red Rocks, Colorado. It's a solid set list, and the band sounds fantastic. You can tell they're all getting along, neither Jerry nor Keith is strung out, and they keep their energy levels high for three gorgeous hours of music: two sets and a meaty encore that includes both their prog-rock-inflected fantasy epic "Terrapin Station" and a cover of Warren Zevon's "Werewolves of London."

I don't know whether Eli ever listened to the show. Maybe he was saving it for later or maybe he had other things on his mind. That was three in the afternoon, Pacific Time, so six o'clock where he was. He probably left his apartment shortly after our conversation; maybe was already out the door by the time I sent the link and didn't want to play a three-hour YouTube video on his phone. It's hard to think of anything that matters less than what I'm wondering about right now, but sometimes I do wonder about it, still.

Here's what I know: Eli was out with friends when he got a text from S, whom he knew through a DIY music venue in Bushwick where they both played shows. S was also the person who had introduced Eli to shooting heroin with a needle, as opposed to taking pills. That night S couldn't find his regular dealer and he wanted Eli—who had a car—to pick him up so they could go see some other dealer he knew. After they scored, Eli dropped off S and then drove back to Red Hook alone, where he shot up in the bathroom of the apartment he shared with three other guys. One of the roommates came home around 2 A.M. and noticed light coming from under the closed door of the bathroom before heading to bed. Eli had overdosed by this point, but was probably still alive. Neither of the other two roommates spent that night at home—one was with his girlfriend; the other, I don't know. When the roommate who was home got up around 4 A.M., presumably to use the bathroom, he found the door still closed and the light still on. When he opened the door he found Eli, but by then it was too late.

The next afternoon I missed a phone call. I was at home in Portland and the phone was sitting beside my laptop on my desk. Everything was exactly as it had been the day before; in fact, it was around the same time of day that I had been tweeting with Eli and Gabe. My phone began to ring and the caller was unknown but the number was a 305 area code. That's Miami, so I reached over to pick it up, half expecting the call to be from a hospital (is Dad okay? is Grandma?), but there was some kind of malfunction: The phone froze and would not let me answer. I tried to call back but the phone wouldn't let me do that either. Then I saw I had a voicemail. I pulled it up. It was another former Pratt student, Anika, and she was crying. Adding to the confusion was the fact that the phone's most recent iOS update had incorporated automatic voice-to-text transcription, but I hadn't gotten a voicemail since installing said update, so I didn't know that I had that feature now. Because it was hard to understand what Anika was saying, I pulled the phone away from my ear to put it on speaker, hoping that this would make it easier to hear. When the screen turned on, it filled with this:

TRANSCRIPTION BETA

"Hey Justin this is Monica um I'm just calling because I didn't want you to find out about the on the Internet um you are I am a little tired I figured I don't know ___ I didn't want you to see it online anyway um I don't how much the fax it I think I left anyway sorry daddy calling with if you feel that are all care . . ."

Was this transcription useful or not useful?

I listened to the message again from the beginning and this time was able to understand.

Like Jason Molina's music, Denis Johnson's story collection, *Jesus' Son,* is a work of art that I had long treasured but felt I was coming to understand in new ways while living in the Midwest, since so much of it takes place in Iowa and Chicago. It's a book about addiction, about just how much despair a life can hold. How arduous and slow, but also how swift and over-mastering, the work of grace can be. It's a book about heroin and an easy one to misunderstand as glamorizing the experience, though for whatever it's worth I don't think that Eli did. I would like to believe that the book gave him a language for articulating to himself those things that he was already struggling with, that it gave him a glimpse of what the path back out might look like, even though it was a path he didn't have the chance to walk.

There are a lot of sad moments in *Jesus' Son,* but the one I come back to the most often, the one that haunts me, is the death of Jack Hotel. In the story "Out on Bail," Hotel and the narrator cop together split the bag, then separate. They both OD but the narrator is revived by his friends while Hotel is not revived by his. The story ends with these lines:

"He died. I am still alive."

This is a book that was taught to me as an undergraduate and as a graduate student, that as a teacher myself now I assign every chance I get. It was on my spring syllabus in Indianapolis, and indeed I had reread and taught it only the week before, on March 16, 2017, to be exact, which it either will or won't surprise you to learn was the fourth anniversary of Jason Molina's death. And I could not, of course, know at that time that Denis Johnson himself would be dead of liver cancer by the end of May.

Jesus' Son has been a part of my life for twenty years and I still find it inexhaustible. Its meanings proliferate and resonate as the years go by. Here's one more layer of meaning it has for me now. In a dream I am back in my classroom at Pratt, it's just me and Eli in the room, he's sitting in one of those awful chair-desks and I'm standing, it's twilight out the window—magic hour—and I am screaming at him the way my father used to scream at me when something was so important that he was willing to blow a vocal cord to make me hear it: the righteous roar of insatiable impotent rage.

I taught you this book, is what I'm screaming. *We talked about it for hours and I made you write a fucking paper on it, then you went and did exactly what it warned you not to do.*

Who would Eli have grown up to be if he'd had the chance to finish growing? Would he have defeated his demon, yoked it and put it to work like Denis Johnson did? Or would his story have gone more like Jason Molina's, who wrote in a song called "Farewell Transmission" these lines that I used to think were metaphorical but which I now understand to be literal:

> *There ain't no end to the sands I've been trying to cross*
> *Real truth about it is*
> *My kind of life is no better off*
> *If it's got the map or if it's lost*

I don't know if those lines are true of Eli. I don't want to believe that they are, that they ever could have been. But I believe they are true of my father, who, though not an addict of any kind, was far more cognizant than he ever let on about the mental illness from which he suffered, and about the ways that depression and rage deformed his life. Like an addict, he white-knuckled it, and predictably enough it worked except for when it didn't. (That it worked as often as it did, for as long as it did, is a testament to his discipline, his enviable and terrifying force of will.) When things fell apart, he did his best to put them back together. This, too, worked except for when it didn't. And then one day it no longer worked at all.

Center Point, Indiana. Off the highway, down the town road, past a church and another church. Long curve around farmland and into the woods. A hilly lane switches from asphalt to gravel, solitary homesteads boasting Trump signs, a swimming hole with a posted notice that says SMILE YOU'RE ON CAMERA and why would it matter to anyone living this far from anywhere whether some kids want to sneak a dip in their mucky pond?

I arrive at the tiger sanctuary just shy of noon. I park in a gravel lot a quarter mile past the main entrance, an employee lot, but a sign says I can also park here. At the far end of the lot, in an industrial garage with its door rolled up, a one-armed employee is using a machete to butcher a cow carcass hanging on a hook.

I walk up the road back the way I drove in, a bucolic quarter mile of two-lane gravel hugged by Indiana woods, to the gate of the sanctuary proper, where my solitude is promptly obliterated by the shouts of a hundred children. This week, I quickly learn, is spring break for some Indiana elementary schools. I pay my $10 admission and get assigned to a tour group. There are about two dozen of us, and I am the only adult other than the tour guide who is not there in his capacity as the guardian of a child.

The tour lasts an hour. Tigers, lions, lynx, and many other big cats; I see them all. The guide tells heartbreaking stories of abuse and rescue. Drug lords and roadside zoos. We watch a feeding (bucket after bucket of chicken quarters) and we hear the lions roar and see the tigers leap from perch to perch in their habitats like the enormous house cats that at this point they basically are. This place does good and difficult and often thankless work. I am glad I gave them my $10, glad I've seen it. I do not have a transformative encounter with the very breathing muscle of wild nature. It is not the best $10 I have ever spent.

The main thing I've gotten out of the visit, I think to myself as I walk back to the car, is the slapstick of my baffled expectation. This will be a lot of fun to tell Dad about. It is just his kind of humor. I almost call him on the ride home— but again I don't. I want to listen to more music, keep thinking things through. Molina and Eli, chance and grace, loss and fate. I want to move *through the static and distance,* as Molina sings near the end of "Farewell Transmission." I want to ride with the ghost again, recover that solitude I forfeited to the sugar-addled elementary school students of Central Indiana. That solitude was what brought me out here, and I need it to carry me back home and so I let it. And that's why I do not call my father, who wouldn't answer the phone if I did call, because he has been dead for a week already, but I won't find that out until tomorrow.

PART II

Everybody Knows This Is Nowhere

The death certificate says March 30. This is not true.

My father died in the kitchen of his apartment in Sunrise Lakes. He probably died of a heart attack, possibly from a stroke, probably on March 24, 2017, though possibly the night before. I know from his phone records that he answered a call from his pharmacy on the afternoon of the twenty-third. He had a new prescription ready and he picked it up. It was Levodopa, the same medication he had been taking for years, but in a new dosage. I do not know whether he tried the new prescription or was waiting for the next day. If he did try it, it is possible—though unlikely—that his death was the result of an adverse reaction to the dosage. The police, having determined that his death was not the result of a crime or intentional self-harm, did not request an autopsy. We were offered the option of having one performed at our own expense. We did not take it.

My last conversation with my father was Sunday, March 19. What did we talk about? The usual stuff: everything and nothing. An upcoming neurologist appointment, my latest failed attempt at admission into the august pages of *The Paris Review*. He probably asked if I'd talked to my sister lately; I probably asked if he'd heard from either of his. I can picture the room I was standing in when I hung up the phone. I guess a part of me is still standing in that room. The sunroom, it was called. The Butler writing program's building is a converted house across the street from the campus proper. I lived as well as taught there. Nights and weekends I had the run of the whole place, and treated it as a kind of extended living room, filling it with music and walking around in my socks. The sunroom is on the ground floor, all wood, big windows on the exterior walls, and the interior wall has built-in bookshelves stocked with the work of faculty and alums and visiting writers and Indiana luminaries: Kurt Vonnegut, Michael Martone, and Booth Tarkington, for whom both my fellowship and the program's literary journal were named. *Booth* magazine. The Booth Tarkington Writer-in-Residence. I am standing in the sunroom forever, phone still warm in my hand;

forever the low moan of the heating system and an SUV bra-
zenly blowing past the Stop sign in front of the campus police
station; forever the dryer-lint light of lingering winter and a
looming afternoon storm.

And then it's eleven days later and the same phone's ringing
and it's Mom. She's crying. She wants to know if I'm alone.

On March 24 or 25, a neighbor with whom Dad was friendly
noticed that she hadn't seen him around. I don't know whether
she tried knocking on his door, though I assume she must
have. If she had done this, and if the blinds on the kitchen
window had been open when she did, she would have seen
his body on the floor. I know she didn't see that because she
let another few days go by. By March 30 she was concerned
enough to call the police, who broke the lock on the door and
found him. They were not sure whom to call. Eventually, they
found phone numbers for my aunt Ronni and for Mom.

Dad's body was taken by the city, sent to the medical examiner, held in a city morgue. My aunts replaced the broken lock

on his door. The apartment, site of a death and some decay, would require professional decontamination before anyone could go inside.

While my mother called my sister, I called my wife. My clearest memory of the night—maybe the only clear one—is her short, high scream when I broke the news. I hear it in my ear as I write this. (Amanda says she does not remember screaming. She says, "I remember saying, 'Oh God' and then sitting in the chair and apologizing to him out loud for failing him." It may be that she said these things after we got off the phone, or that I heard them and simply do not remember. There are good reasons to trust her account over my own. Nevertheless, the only thing I remember about the phone call is the sound that I believe I heard.)

We were all in different places. Amanda was in Portland. Melanie was at home in New York. I was in my campus apartment in Indianapolis. Mom was home in Nashville with her partner, Mark. Dad was in Fort Lauderdale, wherever they had taken him. It was eight or nine o'clock at night, a Thursday. I booked the earliest flight I could get out of Indianapolis the next morning. I told everyone else to stay put. There were more phone calls, made and received.

Baruch dayan ehmet, my friend Joshua said.

Blessed is the true judge.

(Bad Jew that I am, I had to google what it meant.)

I drank whiskey while I packed. This was a shitty tribute to a man who I never once saw take a drink of any alcohol, who despised chemically altered states of all kinds, from drugs and booze to coffee and aspirin, but I wasn't drinking to his memory. I was drinking because I hoped it would help me get enough sleep to wake up in a few hours and drive to the airport. The thing I was doing for him was where I was going—well no, not "for" him, because it was for me, too, but he'd have approved of the decision. If I had called him to ask for advice like I wanted so very, very badly to do just then—Christ, I will never forget that first time, like Mr. Ramsay crying out to his wife in *To the Lighthouse,* that I reached for the phone to call him and he was not there—this is what he would have said. I knew it as plainly as if he'd said it to me: *Justin, you can't help me right now. You'll come when you can come, but for now there's nothing for you to do in Florida. My sisters have each other. You should be with your sister.* He was right, of course. My plane ticket was to JFK.

The endless first night: how I was never going to be able to sleep, but did sleep, waking up every hour or so, seeing dull red 3:30 on the digital clock and remembering, crazily, Dad's story of the alarm at the Nashville airport hotel. My own alarm was set to 5 A.M. I woke up again at 4:57, shut it off, dragged myself to the shower, and hit the road, driving the borrowed Passat through heavy rain in the predawn black. I remember that *Blood on the Tracks* was on the stereo because that's what I'd been listening to while I ran errands the day before. Sobbing, I drove and thought yet again how I am never more my father's son than when I'm behind the wheel of a car with the stereo cranked all the way.

He'd wanted to be a musician at one time, though he didn't play any instruments. I don't know if he ever tried to learn. He always wanted me to learn but I never did. (My sister plays the piano but won't play *for* anybody. It's something she keeps for herself.) He'd had a band in high school, briefly, so briefly that my aunt Francine doesn't even remember it having occurred. He mentioned it to me exactly once. He was the lead singer. He'd had the hair for it back then. (The same long hair *I* grew when I went to college, which he hated.) This would have been 1969, 1970 maybe. Did he write lyrics? I don't know. I know they did Doors covers, may in fact have been exclusively a Doors cover band. He loved Jim Morrison, which when I think about it now is odd to me, because even though he always liked operatic bombast in nearly all its forms other than opera (ELO, King Crimson, Melanie Safka, hair metal, even Barbra Streisand), he loathed mystical mumbo-jumbo of any kind, as well as psychedelic drugs. He considered himself an atheist, a dogmatic realist. He thought it a deep deficiency of both character and intelligence to believe in things you could not see.

It is easy to wish now that I could ask Dad, or that I had asked when I had the chance, what the allure of Morrison was to him, but I doubt he'd have been willing to tell me. He may not have had the words for it himself. I suspect a lot of it was Morrison's voice: the thunderous rumble of the instrument and the total conviction in his delivery, from the louche proposition of "Light My Fire" to the apocalyptic vision quest of "Celebration of the Lizard King." I suspect he was drawn to the total abandon that Morrison embodied, to the idea that if he could have been someone totally unlike himself—a perfect inversion—he might have become something like that.

Another airport, another plane. The canned air of the cabin and cold daylight above the cloud line. Memories surface from the murk of anguish, show themselves, and vanish again. Vivid flashes like animals darting across a road.

In 1994, when I was still acting, I filmed what was to be the opening scene of the Sean Connery film *Just Cause*. I played the lead Boy Scout in a troop that was helping search for a missing girl, Joanie Shriver. We spent four or five days in a swamp, me calling Joanie's name and then finding her mutilated corpse at the base of a tree, Dad watching from the edge of the set. I remember that the swamp was full of bees, and the pale pink nipples on the latex dummy. How I had to poke it with a stick and it rolled over. I had to give the longest, most horrified scream that I could muster. And I did, over and over and over, until I could hardly talk at all: They must have filmed me finding that corpse two dozen times. My parents and I went to see *Just Cause* on opening night. If you've seen this movie you know that the scene I've described does not appear in it. They had replaced my scene with a totally different opening and nobody had told us. "Maybe it'll come later," my mom said. "Like a flashback." We watched the whole shitty, tawdry film in rigid expectation. When it ended, we left the theater in silence. I stormed ahead of them across the parking lot. When I reached the car I started sobbing. I cried so hard

I could barely breathe. My father held me. "We'll get 'em next time," he said, stroking my hair.

Going with him to see Melanie Safka when she played at a nearby Borders Books and Music, I must have been in my senior year of high school, and he was so excited to be in that crowd of a couple dozen people in an overlit room in a chain bookstore that it might as well have been Carnegie Hall. How when she invited requests he asked for "Photograph," his favorite song of hers (*"Do you have a photograph when you were only growing / And your heart was in it?"*) and she told him that she hadn't rehearsed it for this tour, but that it meant a lot to her that he'd asked to hear it, because it rarely got requested, and was a favorite of hers as well.

Or the summer of 2005, when I was living at the Nashville house before moving to New York for grad school—the last time I would ever live at home. I had requested a promo copy of *Tanglewood Numbers*, the new Silver Jews record, and secured an interview with David Berman for *The Brooklyn Rail*. I was sitting in the living room listening to the record over and over on the living-room speakers, the ones Dad had had since college. He sat with me awhile as I listened. I could tell he didn't really like the music, which was somehow both too sedate and too punk for his taste. (After all, this is a guy who thought the best version of "Love Hurts" is the one by Nazareth.) There was one line, though, that jumped out at him. *"Later I come to find / Life is sweeter than Jewish wine,"* Berman sings on "Sleeping Is the Only Love." Dad laughed when he heard this. "That's good," he said, and laughed some more. "That's good."

My sister was waiting for me at her apartment. We sat around crying and laughing, willing seconds into minutes and minutes into hours. We talked about doing a Facebook post. It went against all Dad's preferences, and our own habits too. In the end, we mostly did it because word was spreading. By Friday evening our silence had begun to feel conspicuous; at least to me it did. My sister has Dad's private streak and probably would have ridden the whole thing out in silence. She has a more nuanced understanding of Facebook's privacy controls than anyone I know, and she expressed displeasure more than once that she'd had to share her loss with her colleagues and superiors in order to excuse herself from work. If there'd been any other option I am sure she would have taken it. But there wasn't another option. We hammered out some text and rooted through old photo albums to find pictures we liked—him and me, him and her. We chose old ones, from when we were each small. He was so young and healthy in them—so happy, such a proud dad—that it broke my heart all over again. In a good way, I think. The last few years had been so grim, so densely fogged by suffering, all horizon lines had been obscured. The old pictures were evidence that there had been a time before. The harsh reminder of all we'd lost stood as proof of all we'd had.

People could not understand why we were in New York and not in Florida. Inquiries kept coming about funeral arrangements, a memorial fund. Because he had been so private, and because I—the only person in the family who might be considered a public figure—had rigorously respected that privacy, most people we knew had had no idea he was even sick, much less how sick he'd gotten. We were not yet ready to break the seal on that privacy, and we were certainly not prepared to discuss the specific circumstances of his death, which at that point we ourselves did not fully understand.

Florida law dictated that because his death was not the result of a crime, his physician and not the medical examiner must be the one to sign the death certificate. But he didn't have a GP, just a neurologist to prescribe the Levodopa. The doctor he'd been seeing had retired a month earlier. The new one, the one who'd written the new prescription, saw a potential liability issue and would not sign the certificate, which meant my father's body could not be released to a funeral home. It would end up taking almost three weeks to get him out of the morgue, a Kafkan comedy of bureaucratic horror that was every bit as stupid as it was cruel. But we didn't know then that we had that nightmare ahead of us.

One thing my sister and I did know for sure was that my father would not have wanted a funeral. The idea would have repulsed him: the religiosity, the expense, the pious platitudes offered by people he'd not spoken to in a decade or more, people he felt (in some cases more reasonably than others) had turned their backs on him. I asked my wife to try to explain all this—some sanitized, digestible version of this—to her parents, who had only met him once, some years earlier, but understood his situation well enough. Now they were ready to do whatever was asked of them, go wherever they were needed. They thought Amanda should be where I was, though they did not understand why I was where I was and not where it seemed obvious that both my sister and I ought to have been. I wanted my wife to be with me also. I would have given anything that weekend to put my head in her lap for ten minutes. But I needed her to stay put for the moment, because I knew we would eventually have to go to Florida to clean out his apartment, and I knew I was going to need her then. There are only so many personal days, so many airfare dollars. Being apart had already been terrible and there was nothing we could do. I have no idea what my wife said to her parents but they are good people and she made them understand. They had food delivered to my sister's apartment; my sister-in-law sent a bottle of whiskey with which to wash it down.

Replies to the Facebook post came from people I'd grown up with but did not necessarily know well. Some I was never even properly "friends" with. I doubt I ever had their phone number or saw the inside of their house. They remembered Larry Taylor as a Little League coach. As a fundraiser for the debate team, the Hebrew school. As someone who helped them write an important speech—the valedictorian told me this—when her own parents couldn't. The kids who had been my childhood friends remembered trips to Grand Prix, the enormous video arcade in the cruddy part of Hollywood. To Jaxson's Ice Cream Parlor in Dania Beach, a kitsch tourist trap to which Dad had been going since he'd moved to

Florida in 1969 (a stone's throw, in those days, from the Pirates World amusement park). He'd been taking my sister and me to Jaxson's since we were kids.

Amanda's friend Becky is a social worker, one of a very few friends of ours who knew my father's full situation because I'd relied on her at times for counsel, and she'd given generously of her expertise. Becky wanted to make a donation to a charity in Dad's name. Did I have one in mind? I didn't. My sister and I started looking up Parkinson's charities but we didn't know how to vet them. Then I had a better idea. Take the money, I told Becky, and go spend it on your kids. Take them to the movies and out for ice cream. Get the extra toppings. That's who our father was. When he was healthy, when he was his best self. He volunteered to do the late pickups that the other parents tried to weasel out of: from the movie, the bar mitzvah, whatever. When I was twelve and thirteen years old, just old enough to want to go see grunge shows at scuzzy nightclubs but too young to be left alone in such places, he bought himself a ticket and went with me and my friends. We saw the Foo Fighters and the Presidents of the United States of America at a nightclub in Fort Lauderdale; it was each band's first tour. We saw Radiohead open for R.E.M. at the Miami Arena. The Vandals, Cake, and No Doubt on a triple bill at Coral Sky Amphitheatre. Dad was a little disappointed, I think, when we got old enough to go on our own, because he liked spending time with us and he genuinely enjoyed going to the shows. They weren't always the shows he would have chosen (he and I on our own saw Aerosmith; we saw Billy Joel) but he liked to see the new bands from right up close, and to know—for his own peace of mind as much as ours— that he was there if we needed him. He chaperoned, he treated. There was always room to fit one more kid in his car.

Here's a Jaxson's story: One time Dad was doing late pickup duty after a bat mitzvah. There was palpable disappointment in the car, a consensus that the party had been subpar. (Why? Who knows. The way young suburban Jews are habituated to the insane standards of the average bar/bat mitzvah party, and the perverse class judgments this engenders, is a subject for another time.) There were four, maybe five of us in the car. We dropped off the first kid, Jeffrey, at home as planned. I floated the suggestion that we go to Jaxson's as a sort of consolation for the letdown of the party, and Dad said sure. My friend Menal (she still remembers this) said there was no way her parents would let her do that. It was already past ten o'clock and she was expected home. Menal's parents were much more strict with her than most of the rest of us were used to, and this was the pre–cell phone era, so it wasn't like she could send them an updated plan. Dad offered to petition them on her behalf. We all went inside and a great negotiation ensued. When all of Menal's father's other objections had been answered, he played what I assume he thought was his trump card: that it wouldn't be fair if Menal got to go and her little brother, Rajiv, did not. My father understood this not as an insurmountable obstacle but rather as the two of them having finally come to agreement. Of course Rajiv could come get ice cream! Tell him to get dressed and let's go before it gets any later.

Dad loved telling this story, which has two punch lines. The first one is about young Rajiv, who'd have been ten or eleven at the time, dragged out into the night with a carload of his sister's friends to an ice-cream parlor two towns over from where we all lived. He was overwhelmed by the whole Jaxson's shtick: the old-fashioned candy-store theme, the heaping bowls of greasy popcorn waiting at the table when you sat down, the seemingly endless menu. While the rest of us compared various complicated sundaes, weighed the wisdom of a quart-size milkshake, Rajiv settled on vanilla ice cream with no toppings, to be served in a dish. Dad, incredulous, begged him to reconsider. "Try something else," Dad said. "Anything else. I promise I'll get you the vanilla if you don't like it." But Rajiv was determined to get vanilla ice cream in a dish with no toppings; the only concession he made was to a plain waffle cone, provided it was presented as a side to the dish of ice cream. So that's what Rajiv got, and every time Dad retold this story for the next twenty-plus years he was just as gobsmacked as he had been on the night that it happened. The story never failed to crack him up.

The second punch line isn't really a punch line, I guess, but it says something crucial about Dad. It's *my* kicker to this story when I tell it as a story about him. Dad never got over the fact that we only thought to make the Jaxson's trip after dropping off Jeffrey at home, and that by the time we brokered the deal with Menal's parents it was too late at night to go back to Jeffrey's house and attempt to fetch him. The exclusion of Jeffrey offended his sense of fairness, and he held himself responsible for it. He always ended the Jaxson's story by mentioning that he still felt bad about Jeffrey not getting to go.

The last time I heard him tell this story would have been in late 2014 or early 2015. He was finally set up at the apartment in Sunrise Lakes, and Amanda and I had come down for a visit. We took him to Jaxson's, on the pretext that Amanda wanted to see it, or maybe that I wanted to show it to her. And both those reasons were true but neither was the real reason. I wanted to take him there. I wanted to buy him the biggest silliest dish of ice cream I could talk him into ordering, and I wanted to pay for it for once, and I wanted Amanda to hear him tell the story, which, as if on cue, he launched into as soon as we sat down.

Larry Taylor's defining quality was his intensity. He was intensely intelligent and inquisitive; he was intensely competitive and intensely generous. His anger was unpredictable and, once triggered, impossible to contain. He was never physically violent but he could (I think without meaning to) present as menacing. There were arguments with waiters that ended up ruining birthday dinners; shouting and tears in public places. But he was also a willing, empathetic listener. People trusted him with their deepest, darkest secrets. He was a capacious absorber of information and a great giver of advice.

When he was in one of his rages it was as though the whole world fell away and all he saw was his own anger like a red blind over his eyes. But when you asked him for help it was as though, again, the whole world fell away and all he saw was you, and what you saw, and all he wanted was to solve the problem. It didn't matter whether the issue was which pair of shoes to buy or the defense strategy at your upcoming trial. It didn't matter whether the discussion took ten minutes or ten hours: He was there for it.

He was almost totally incapable of advocating for himself or experiencing pleasure and satisfaction on his own behalf. He overinvested in people because his deepest joys were vicarious; he tried to keep his sorrow and rage to himself but did not know how. He thought of himself as a loner, as antisocial, as a curmudgeon, but in fact he desperately needed people. Their validation and especially their need of him. Like anyone, he craved love, but he doubted he deserved it and in some ways I think he thought himself weak for needing it, for not being the rock and island of the old Simon & Garfunkel song, which he loved, and whose lyrics I do not believe he ever read as intended, which is to say as a tragedy, a self-betraying howl of grief. He heard the sadness there, but still thought the song described a plausible way to live your life.

He had a great sense of humor and no sense of irony. When he hurt people, he knew it and felt bad about what he'd done. When he apologized, he meant it. When he hurt himself, on the other hand, he was unforgiving, and therefore unforgiven. It would have been difficult, perhaps impossible, for most people to match the intensity he presented, to give him back what he gave them.

Some people loved him and some hated him. Some thought he was an asshole, or nuts, or their best friend, or their hero, or all of the above. But there was one thing that everyone who knew him said about him. They said that they had never known anyone else like him in their whole lives.

My father's funeral took place the Sunday of my visit to New York City: April 2, 2017. Only my sister and I were there for it. We didn't know that was what we were doing at the time, but I understand now that it's what we did.

We had spent the previous day attempting to navigate some of the miserable death bureaucracy that we did not yet know would swallow much of the following month. We had mourned with cousin Michael, who lives with his wife and daughters in Tribeca. We were feeling restive, cooped-up. It had been a cold, rainy weekend, but on Sunday it was sunny and clear.

Melanie lived in Hell's Kitchen, so I suggested that we take the 1 train up to Morningside Heights. I'd spent a lot of time there during my New York years. My first apartment in the city had been on 107th and Amsterdam. After my first book came out, I was offered a class at the Columbia MFA program: my first academic assignment outside of the comp department. Telling my parents that I'd be teaching at Columbia was in some ways as great a moment as when I'd told them I sold the book.

When I was a high school senior there had been some disappointment about my "settling" for a state school; I had

145

good enough grades to shoot higher but my parents were basically broke. There was at that time in Florida a lottery-funded scholarship program to any in-state public university, and I automatically qualified for a full ride on account of my GPA. My mom thought I ought to at least apply to Brown, my dream school. (The only thing I knew about it was that they supposedly didn't have grades; thank God I hadn't heard of Hampshire.) She also wanted me to apply to Columbia, which for some reason had become the brightest star in the firmament of the family's educational imaginary: the fanciest, most important school you could get into. (It was where Menal was going.) Dad thought I should live at home for two years, get a job, go to Florida Atlantic or some other local place. I could save up money, see how things went.

University of Florida had been a way of splitting the difference. It was the best school in the state, public or private, and I would surely get in if I applied. I didn't want to take out massive loans and, as a matter of more immediate concern, didn't want to be bothered filling out long applications, writing essays. I was ambitious but lazy. The application to UF was a single page, no essay, and I could do it online, which was still a novelty back then. I think it took me ten minutes. I applied for both early decision and early admission, to start the summer before my freshman fall. I was ready to get out of the house. They took me and I went.

To soothe my parents' residual fears and ease their guilt about the way things had gone, I said something so crazy only a high school senior could ever have thought to say it. I told them not to worry that I wasn't going to Columbia because in ten years' time I'd be teaching there.

I said this and immediately forgot about it, but circumstance conspired to make it come true almost to the day. My mother, ecstatic, reminded me of my own brash prophecy, and so Columbia has always been a special place for me.

Say what you will about the adjunct grind, about labor exploitation in the academy, about the psychic trauma (economic violence and class shame) that leads to the outsize veneration of such an institution in the first place, but Columbia was good to me. I liked my students and my colleagues and always felt at home there. When I go back to the city to visit I always find a few hours to go up to campus, walk across the quad, proceed to the Hungarian Pastry Shop on 111th and Amsterdam, and then across the street to the Church of Saint John the Divine. Sometimes I go inside the church but usually I sit by the oxidized copper statue of the Archangel Michael. He's beheading the devil with his sword while giraffes frolic around him and they're all riding the broad back of a crab that is itself rising on a column of water from the formless deep.

It is a favorite place of mine, this park and statue, but more than that, a kind of holy place (I mean this separately from its status as the grounds of a church). This was where I went to think, to read, to write. I was in this park when I called my future father-in-law to ask permission to propose to his daughter. I have spent hundreds of hours there, many of them on the phone with my father, his voice huge in my ears to drown out the traffic, me sipping coffee on a shaded bench or circling the statue at a slow clip, as we talk and talk and talk.

I wanted to share this with my sister. I took her on my little circuit: campus, coffee shop, park. We sat with our cookies and coffee by the statue and soaked up the sun and remembered our father. After a while we got restless and so walked to the northwest corner of Central Park and entered it and started south and, without quite deciding to do so, walked its whole length over the course of a perfect New York spring afternoon that eased into evening, walking and talking for hours, the two of us.

I'm not going to get into what we talked about: That's just ours. But it was without question what my father would have wanted, and the finest memorial I could have imagined for him: a conversation. He was with us in the intensity of our missing him, of our needing him and of his not being there, of our finding each other instead. He would have expected no less of us and at the same time would not have wanted or condoned anything more. As far as he was concerned, there never was anything more than this to hope for: a happy family, kids who love each other and love him and know, too, that they are loved, forever and no matter what. That's not inference; these are things that he told me, that we talked about many times over the years.

Walking and talking, often about him but also just as often about other things, we began to comprehend the size of our loss—the terrain of it—and at the same time to chart a path through. We continue, together and apart, to make our way.

Hattiesburg Notebook

I'm driving from Hattiesburg, Mississippi, down to New Orleans to visit my friend Jami when it occurs to me to call my father. I've got ninety good driving minutes ahead of me, a perfect amount of time to give him. Question is, can I reach the phone where it's mounted on the dash cradle, pull up his number in my contacts, make it dial, and do all this with one finger and without taking my eyes off the road? Maybe. But it doesn't matter because I won't make the attempt because there is no call to make because there is no one to receive it. This is Dad's car I'm driving, the 2007 Nissan Sentra that I inherited when he died five months ago.

I would not say that I "forgot" all this, but rather that, as an ex-smoker reaches by reflex for his absent pack, or an amputee's sharpest pain is in the very void of the missing limb, the act of burning through hours of downtime with an aimless phone call to my old man has been such a central part of my life for so long that it is more than merely instinctual to reach for the phone. *Shooting the shit with Dad* is a part of who I am or who I was or who we were or all of these. It will be a slow unlearning, an excruciating resignation to this everlasting fact of silence, even as there is in that same silence the booming calm of suffering abated, the eerie peace of armistice after a long and fruitless war.

It's late August 2017. I've been in Hattiesburg for three weeks and I still don't know where anything is. The school didn't have housing to offer me, and though I could have afforded to rent my own apartment (or even house!), after Indianapolis I was reluctant to live alone again, so I rented a room in a house whose other occupants are an alumna of the program where I teach and a woman who works at the local paper. I needed Google Maps to give me directions from my house to the on-ramp to 59 South. From there it was a straight shot down to the I-10 junction. I'll take I-10 west to New Orleans, exit at Elysian Fields, pull the map back up at the first red light I hit, and verify the last couple of turns that'll take me to Jami's place.

For now, though, I can unplug the phone and switch over to the CD player. It's a six-disc changer, and five of the discs in there are mine, high school and college stuff, dug out of my basement back in Portland on the day before I left—but the sixth disc is a CD-R copy of the Rolling Stones' *Beggars*

Banquet that I found in a paper sleeve in the Nissan's center console, labeled in Dad's supremely disciplined script with a fine-point Sharpie that I can picture in the cup of pens that used to sit on his desk. I put the CD in the changer as soon as I found it and I haven't taken it out since. *Beggars Banquet* is what I put on now. I turn the volume up. I'll keep the windows down until the rain comes.

Before it was my father's car it was my sister's. My parents got it for her and she used it during college, then for another year or two after. Melanie gave it to Dad when she moved to DC for law school. He always said she could reclaim it whenever she wanted, but she went from DC to New York to begin her career, and we all knew she was never going to ask for it back. When Dad died the car was jointly inherited by my sister and me, but because he didn't leave a will, "the estate" (such as it was) had to go through Florida probate court before we could do anything with it. She told me to take it if I wanted it; I said I didn't. Amanda and I had just leased a car in Portland, and one for us to share was plenty. The Passat, of course, had been returned to my mom's friend's kid when the gig in Indianapolis ended.

Melanie and I had been looking into donating the car to a children's charity, but by the time we got through with probate I had been offered this job in Mississippi, indeed had spent half a day on the Internet trying to figure out if I should get a short-term lease or buy a used clunker to get me through the school year, when it dawned on me that I already owned a car.

I had the Nissan shipped from Sunrise to Gulf Breeze (a suburb of Pensacola), where my in-laws lived. My father-in-law received the vehicle on my behalf, put in a new battery, and had the oil changed. I flew in from Portland on August 8. My wife and I go visit every Christmas, and for a week most summers: We had just been there in June. It felt bizarre to be taking that flight a second time so soon, and without her there.

In the car I found an umbrella, a reflective silver sun-shield, and a roll of paper towels. I kept those. I threw out an old thermos that I recognized from my own childhood, and would not have dared open. I threw out faded maps of Nash-ville and Miami. I did not want to throw out his North Miami Beach Optimist Club ball cap, yellow letters on black foam, a mesh back. This had been his baseball-coaching hat, one of them anyway, and for the last several years his go-to for when he was driving and the sun was in his eyes. It was sitting on the passenger seat: ancient, dusty, stinky from sitting inside the closed-up car between March and now. I wanted to find a way to salvage that hat, to put it on my own head and drive around wearing it, though I recognized in my desire to make this gesture something of Dad's own intense sentimental streak, an erring on the side of preservation that I had often found frustrating and at times creepy. I imagined my wife see-ing me wearing the hat, her palpable discomfort—at the fetish aspect, sure, but also at the undeniable fact of it being old and gross, which I'd told Dad myself any number of times. But she was back home and so that didn't factor, or not imme-diately. What I wanted, more than anything, was to drive to

Mississippi wearing the hat, and let him make the trip with me that way. I would throw it away when I got there. That seemed like a reasonable compromise, right?

I heard his voice in my head, clear and sharp as he ever was in his heyday, in my childhood: *Let's not bullshit each other, Justin. If you don't throw it out now you're never going to throw it out, so make a decision and let's get on with our lives.*

I threw out the hat. A few minutes later I found *Beggars Banquet*. It was with two other CDs, neither of which could have been his. One was the soundtrack to the Beatles-inspired musical *Across the Universe*; the other was the first disc of a Dave Matthews Band double live album. These must have been my sister's leave-behinds, and he—characteristically— would not have thrown them out, because what if she wanted them back someday? I sent a picture of the discs to my sister, who was suitably amused.

I thought about sending her a picture of the hat too but that seemed sad, and anyway I'd already thrown it out. *Beggars Banquet*, as mentioned, went straight into the changer. Dave Matthews and the movie soundtrack went back into the paper sleeve, which went back into the console. I have never listened to them. I will never throw them out.

I drove to Hattiesburg with an expired Florida tag and upon arrival attempted to register the car there. It turned out that since the probate court had determined us to be joint owners of all of our father's possessions, my sister either needed to present herself at the Hattiesburg tax assessor's office to put her name on the title, or else she had to grant me limited power of attorney in order to transfer the title to me exclusively. This she did. "The Nissan," I texted her, "has officially experienced the least likely of all its possible fates: a Mississippi license plate." I attached a photograph. "Well there's a thing I never thought I'd see," she replied.

I had a month left in Indianapolis when Dad died, and the end of that semester was a blur, a fugue. New York to see my sister; Portland, Maine, to present a paper at a conference (I thought about canceling, but Dad would have disapproved); South Florida, where I rendezvoused with my sister and my wife, to see my aunts and grandparents, to clean out Dad's apartment, and to begin the process of settling his affairs. In between each of these trips I went back to Indianapolis to teach. During the month of April 2017 I was on a plane every third or fourth day. The chair of the writing program had suggested I cancel classes, but I refused to do this. It felt better to keep moving, to have work to do, and the prospect of making up those classes at the end of the term, of extending my stay in Indianapolis, was more odious than teaching through my jet lag and grief.

I got back to Portland on the first of May. On the ninth of May I got an email out of the blue, inviting me to apply for another visiting writer position, this one in the PhD program at the University of Southern Mississippi. I had not planned to apply for anything else in 2017, indeed had been looking forward to a return to self-employment—in other words, to being a house husband. To staying home and licking my wounds. I'd promised myself while in Indianapolis that I was never again going to complain about having to go to the grocery store because my wife was at the office all day: I would just be grateful to have a wife with whom to eat dinner every night. But the Southern Miss job was an attractive one. Amanda and I had several long talks about it. It was a tough decision, and we really didn't want to do the long-distance thing again, but we were trying to buy a house in Portland and getting outbid over and over, so if I took the job and saved a decent chunk of what I made down there . . .

We all know the words to this song. The pros and cons on our list were exactly what you'd think they were, and they aren't the point of this story. We decided I'd take the job, and with that decision the summer of 2017 turned into a kind of shore leave, the restful stretch between lonely tours of duty.

I hate that Dad does not know, can never know, that I got this job: the 2017–2018 artist-in-residence of the University of Southern Mississippi PhD in creative writing. Just the kind of title he would crow over.

He will never ask me how the students are and he will never scoff when I insist that Mississippi's not so bad, or at least not all bad. *No, Dad, really.* I will never be obliged to explain why boiled peanuts are awesome or to tell him that he's being an asshole when he goes on and on about the Bible-thumping sister-fucking rednecks and Trump-voting Nazi scum—*Jew-haters, every one of them*—and I'll never get to tell him that I see far more bumper stickers for Bernie Sanders than for Clinton and Trump combined.

It's not that Dad would be wrong exactly, about the South, where even as I write these lines I can see thunderheads menacing the small group of Confederate loyalists protesting out by the school's front gate for the restoration of the Battle Flag to the state flag. They've been out there every weekend for one hundred weeks and counting, someone told me, ever since—surprise—the university got its first black president. So yes, the South is what it is. It is the worst thing you might think about it. But it isn't *only* that.

He would not believe me but he would hear me out, listen and raise objections, scold me on my naïveté, and this—the un-had argument—is what I'm mourning. The heated parrying, the talking too fast, points and subpoints and digressions, talking over each other. Our shared pastime, our common tongue.

This is the first time I've ever lived in the Deep South. Now, I know what you're thinking: *Wait, didn't you grow up in Miami and didn't you go to college in Gainesville?* Yes and yes. But as I'm sure some of you already know, and the rest of you will never fully understand, Florida's status as a Southern state is hotly, permanently contested. Everything south of Disney World is basically considered part of New York. Everything above is granted Southern, but not *Deep Southern* status. The Deep South doesn't start until you either get west of

Tallahassee or hit the Georgia state line. (Tennessee isn't part of the Deep South either; it's too far north.)

That said, Hattiesburg and Gainesville remind me of each other. Sure there are differences: Hattiesburg is a much smaller town and Southern Miss is a much smaller school than University of Florida. Hattiesburg's ragged edges are more ragged; the barbecue is better but the coffee is worse. And things are different for me too: I'm a professor, not a student; I'm thirty-five, not nineteen. And yet I live on a shady street in a slightly shabby neighborhood a lot like the one where I lived in Gainesville, in a house that reminds me of the old house, in a bedroom that is so similar to my college bedroom (down to the wood-crate bookshelf and Grateful Dead poster) it sometimes feels like I fell down a rabbit hole and landed in my own past.

My freshman year at the University of Florida I lived in an honors dorm with a friend from my hometown. He was a pre-med student who wanted badly to switch his major to music but was afraid to disappoint his parents. He spent that year studying hard science that he hated and playing an online RPG. He sometimes hung out with me and my new friends, but mostly I think we terrified him. We were all aspiring artists of some kind or another, and though the core friend-group was all students, we were less interested in the university scene than in the local punk and activist communities, which themselves overlapped and put us into the orbits of still more marginal people:

squatters, train hoppers, gutter punks, other castaways and survivors. These were people who had, for whatever reason, abandoned their so-called normal lives, or had been kicked out of them, or (in a lot of cases) never had remotely normal lives to begin with, and were living the only way that made sense to them, though to most people (my parents, for instance, or my roommate) they registered as weirdos and petty criminals, which needless to say some of them also were. From the tender and damaged to the conniving and deranged, these people were free in a way that we had never before encountered, and some of them became part of the new community that we were building for ourselves.

When summer hit I found a part-time job fundraising for the university and moved with a couple of like-minded guys into a house a few blocks off-campus. The house was christened "Abraham," after the old Sunday school song that goes, *"Father Abraham had many sons / many sons had father Abraham."*

Abraham had previously been the home of a local jam band, so it was pretty much wrecked when we inherited it. That suited us fine. The house was a base for friends, activists, and sundry travelers. Food Not Bombs would come over and cook sometimes. One guy lived in his van in the backyard. A couple shared a VW bus out front. Another friend, though she'd stayed in the dorms a second year, had a tent set up on the side of the house as a sort of gutter pied-à-terre. People would drop by for a beer and end up staying for days.

This was the beginning of a time in my life—two years, give or take—when for me and a handful of my closest friends, there weren't necessarily clear lines where any one person ended and another began. It was like experience itself had been, in the Deleuzian sense, de-territorialized. The best I can liken it to is what Freud, in *Civilization and Its Discontents,* calls "the oceanic feeling." It's a sense of being at one with the universe. This feeling, and the desire to achieve it, is consistent across all religions throughout the world and throughout history, so much so that it seems to be the precondition for religion itself. Freud goes on to say that he has never felt this feeling. I imagine most people don't want to, and fewer still ever get the chance.

My parents came up from Miami to visit in what must have been July or August of 2001. I tried to convince them not to, but despite my objections (or, more likely, because of them) they were determined to see this house for themselves and help me get settled. They arrived a couple of hours earlier than expected, and so found me barely awake, viciously hungover. The front door was hanging open and they were bade welcome by a man with long tangled hair and an Old Testament beard, who was sweeping leaves out of the living room and into the yard. This was C, an ex-Mormon turned latter-day flower child turned accidental hobo after he got evicted from his apartment, at which point he started a rotation of friends' couches, which over the ensuing months would narrow to mostly just our couch. An alcoholic to the point of incontinence, he'd taken to wearing bathing suits instead of regular shorts because they were easier to handwash after he inevitably pissed himself while sleeping. (Needless to say, but he also washed a lot of couch cushions.) His daily routine was to do a few chores around the house to earn his keep, then go steal a case of beer from a grocery store. (A

case? A case. He had a system. I don't know what it was.)
He'd bring the case of beer back to Abraham and work his
way through it while he read philosophy until those of us with
jobs and/or classes were done with them and could come
home to drink with him. That is: He drank until it was time to
start drinking. C was basically a Denis Johnson character:
well-meaning, weak-willed, regularly blessed with epiphanies
from which he failed to gain anything.

C was, as I said, sweeping leaves out of the living room
when my parents arrived at the house. The reason that the
living room was full of leaves was that neither the front door
nor the back door nor any of the windows had been closed in
days.

The visit did not go well. When my mother saw the state
of my bedroom, she cried. Instead of a bed I had this big gross
oval cushion my friend Friedel had found for me at a garage
sale for a dollar. It was stained and had no sheets on it. My
parents wanted to take me to buy a bed but I wouldn't hear of
such bourgeois pretension. I knew people who could live for
three months on what a bed cost! Why not just give the money
to them? Or better still, give it to me and I'll live on it.

The whole day went like this. We somehow ended up at a
Best Buy, where I consented to have some extension cords
and a CD tower purchased on my behalf. Dad, I remember,
had become obsessed with the problem of electrical cords left
out where people could trip on them, and he had a plan—
which he duly executed—to set things up so all cords were
run flush to baseboards. They left the next day, and not too
long afterward I got a letter in the mail from Dad: four single-
spaced pages in which he detailed his disappointment in me,

his outrage and disgust at the way I was living, and his culmi-
nating demand that I change my life or else.

I'm not sure what he meant the *or else* to be, since there
was not much money to cut me off from. My tuition was paid
for by a state scholarship; my living expenses were covered by
my part-time job and the dregs of my child acting money.
Given my lifestyle, said expenses rarely amounted to $500 a
month, including rent. More to the point, he would never
have gone through with any threat that cut us off from each
other. It was too close to the kind of shit his own parents had
put him through. Also, as someone who really had supported
himself, who knew what it meant to be entirely self-sufficient,
he knew that I was utterly incapable of doing what he had
done. I wasn't going to work at a door factory. I didn't even
know how to drive a car!

If he had emailed me, I would have emailed him back, and
though this was a few years before Gmail, there's some chance
I'd have a record of what was said. Instead, faced with the
seemingly insurmountable prospect of finding a stamp and an
envelope, I called him. We had yet another blowout, eventually coming to yet another détente. I kept my grades up,
played the good son during phone calls and visits home as
best I could, and sought transcendence and fought the class
war on my own time. Dad did not visit Gainesville again until
after I graduated: the summer of 2004. He picked me up in a
Ryder truck loaded with all the stuff from our house in Miami,

which had just been sold. To this I added two or three boxes' worth of books, CDs, and clothes. We drove toward Nashville, stopping for the night in Warner Robins, Georgia, which Dad picked because it was slightly more than halfway there: We could light out early, hit Nashville by lunchtime. We couldn't know this then, but just as the letter he sent me in 2001 became the model for the one I sent him in 2007, this drive in 2004 was the same one we would take ten years later, albeit in reverse, when I was tasked with getting him out of Nashville and bringing him back home.

Not long after that disastrous visit, I sent my father what would turn out to be his favorite gift I ever gave him: a paperback book called *The Jesus Mysteries*, by Timothy Freke and Peter Gandy, a somewhat dubious work of pop history which seeks to prove that the historical Jesus Christ never existed, that his story was only a patchwork of pagan folktales and Greek mythology tacked onto a rumor and a political movement. He read the book several times and talked about it often: how the authors hoisted Christianity by its own petard of hypocrisy and bullshit. The only books on his shelf in his last apartment were the books that I have written or edited; an illustrated book of Jewish prayers, which he'd had since his own childhood; and *The Jesus Mysteries*.

I couldn't tell him that I came across *The Jesus Mysteries* in the course of learning about Gnosticism, which—precisely because it was a heresy—seemed safer to admit I was interested in than Christianity as such. Eventually I moved on to the real stuff, and for a few years flirted with the prospect of converting.

My frustration with Judaism was not what it demanded of me, but rather with my perception that it did not demand enough. It seemed abstract and bloodless and life-denying and hopelessly bourgeois. I'm well enough read now to know that all these charges are more or less identical with those levied against Christianity by Nietzsche and D. H. Lawrence, among countless others. My critiques were not nearly as specific to Judaism as I thought they were at the time. They were, for the most part, an angsty, artsy teenager's critiques of bourgeois institutions as such. You could press the same charges against any religion whose role as a vector of culture has over time come to supplant its original purpose, and thereby semi-secularized it, smoothing the *faith* out of "the faith" until you're left with the spiritual equivalent of sea glass.

But I was enough of an innocent—and, despite my best efforts otherwise, enough of a Jew—to not know any of this before I left for college, where along with the usual things you expect college students to experiment with, I found the freedom to follow my spiritual instincts wherever they might take me. This quest became deeply intertwined with the aesthetic and political reinventions I was undergoing at the same time. I took a class on the history of apocalyptic thought where we read Norman Cohn's *The Pursuit of the Millennium: Revolutionary Millenarians and Mystical Anarchists of the Middle Ages* and other works of Marxist historicism. These texts suggested a moral and historical continuity with the anarchist-activist-DIY scene that I had become involved with.

A lot of the people in that scene had dropped out of school, or had never gone in the first place. I thought about dropping out myself sometimes, but not seriously. I loved being a student. It never ceased to amaze and slightly stupefy me that I could just pick whatever I wanted to know about—from queer theory to Shakespeare, from modernism to creative writing—and some expert would show up and tell me everything he or she knew about it. It *still* blows my mind that the system works this way, and this perhaps more than any other reason is why I so love being a teacher. You never know which book on your syllabus is going to be the one that changes a mind or a life, but you always know that any of them can.

In a poetry workshop I took in my sophomore year we were assigned Gjertrud Schnackenberg's *Supernatural Love.* I still have my copy of that book, so I can see all of my old notes. The most embarrassing and emblematic piece of marginalia is at the opening of the poem "Darwin in 1881." Schnackenberg writes: "Sleepless as Prospero back in his bedroom / In Milan, with all his miracles / Reduced to sailors' tales / He sits up in the dark." The underlining is mine and next to it I have written "and Jesus was a sailor . . ." because I understood a trope was being drawn upon here but the only other text I knew in which Christ is associated with the sea was Leonard Cohen's song "Suzanne" (Cohen himself having been at that time another fairly recent discovery).

Clearly, I was reinventing every wheel I came across.

Moreover, my literary, spiritual, and political educations were functionally indistinct from one another. I was happy to abide in paradoxes. I devoured Chesterton's *Orthodoxy* but also Bataille's *Accursed Share*; Marilynne Robinson's *The Death of Adam* meant no less to me than Hakim Bey's *Temporary Autonomous Zone*.

My novel, *The Gospel of Anarchy*, which came out in 2011, was my attempt to capture both the ecstasy and the entropy of the Gainesville years. One of the novel's central ideas is that Christianity and anarchism are two streams from a common spring, because they both evince an ethos of radical emancipation. The novel also attempts to reckon with Kierkegaard's exegesis of the sacrifice of Isaac in *Fear and Trembling*. I was for a long time fascinated by the argument that Abraham, obeying God, must nonetheless be considered a murderer, even though his willingness to kill his son is the result of his unshakeable faith. There can be no exception made for Abraham, insists Kierkegaard, notwithstanding that he obeys an order higher than the law, nor that the deed was never done, but only *would have been done* had God not commanded him to stop, even as He had first commanded him to proceed. The deed is in the will and so too the sin. The highest devotion, says Kierkegaard, is to break God's own law out of love for God and then to suffer the consequences of having committed the transgression, so that the sanctity of God's law is upheld even as it is violated on God's command.

This reading is in keeping with the classical Christian notion that the God of the Old Testament is the God of Law, whereas the God of the New Testament is the God of Love. It's not hard to see why Jews might resent the idea that their God does not love them, why they might consider such an assertion to be an anti-Semitic canard. Except I didn't see it, not then. It was the experience of writing the novel, and then of having to live with having written it, that precipitated a different reckoning: I was forced to confront the fact that I knew next to nothing about the faith in which I was ostensibly raised.

I had, for far too long, blamed others for this blank spot on my spiritual-intellectual map: my parents, my Hebrew school, American Judaism's understanding of itself as a primarily secular-cultural rather than religious-spiritual tradition. But the question of whether or to what degree my blame was justly assigned only served to obscure the fact that the act of blame itself was backward-looking and useless. I had invented a Christianity for myself when I'd needed one, hadn't I? Why shouldn't I invent a Judaism too?

The work is ongoing: Bellow, Ozick, Kafka, Scholem; Alter, Buber, Heschel, Paley, Cole. On and on. And whatever else it is or may become, this work is first and foremost a literary undertaking. In Abraham Heschel's *The Prophets,* in a chapter called "The Theology of Pathos," I find an exegesis of the Isaac story to rival Kierkegaard's. Heschel writes that "Man is not only an image of God; he is a perpetual concern of God. Man is a consort, a partner, a factor in the life of God." Therefore, "It was because of the experience of God's responding to him in his plea for Sodom that Abraham did not question the command to sacrifice his only son." For Heschel, the question of

God's law is secondary to that of God's *personality*. Abraham knows God the way one knows a spouse or a best friend. He judges God trustworthy and it turns out his trust is well founded.

A factor in the life of God.

Isn't that beautiful? I love it. I wish I'd known about it ten years ago, when I was writing my novel. On the other hand, the version of me who knew his Heschel ten years ago wouldn't have needed to write *The Gospel of Anarchy* in the first place. He might not have read Kierkegaard at all, and he certainly never would have met the people who turned out to be some of the best friends he ever had.

It's a pretty safe bet at this point that I'm not going to convert to Christianity, but the life, work, and example of Christ still have meaning and weight to me. His radical and boundless love; his politics of universal emancipation and inclusion; his belief that in order to fully understand what it meant to be human he had to experience not merely suffering, but forsakenness. That to know what it is to be us he had to know what we feel when we call out for him and he is not there. At a guess I'd say I'm as much a Christian as Leonard Cohen ever was. And I'm coming to understand something that I believe Cohen knew: Whatever else your Christophilia does for you, it will not relieve either the complexity or the urgency of the question of what it means to be a Jew.

"Knowledge increases unreality," writes Gjertrud Schnackenberg in "Darwin in 1881." It is the last line of the first stanza, just a dozen lines down from the passage I quoted earlier. I was smart enough, at nineteen years old, to underline the sentence. What took a long time was learning to read it.

Earlier, when I told the story of my trip to New York in April right after Dad died, there was one part that I left out, because it didn't fit with the way that I wanted to end the chapter: that portrait of me and my sister walking off into the sunset in Central Park. Because life is not a story—it's just what we make stories out of—there is no last page as long as we are still living it, and so it keeps happening after you stop reading the book, after the writer stops writing it. What happened after our walk was nothing special, which is another reason that I left it out. My sister and I went back to her apartment, ordered dinner, drank the whiskey my sister-in-law had sent us. We watched TV and griped about the president. My flight to Indianapolis was late Monday afternoon out of JFK. We woke up the next morning and had breakfast. My sister had taken the day off work, was talking about going to the gym, maybe cleaning her apartment. Getting back to her life, or at any rate starting to try. We said our goodbyes and I left, but it was too early to head to the airport yet. I took the subway to Fort Greene to get coffee with Anika.

Anika is two or three years younger than Eli. His cohort were juniors when she started at Pratt. I had Anika in my freshman writing studio and I was impressed with her right from the start. She was a smart reader and a strong writer. We were from the same part of Florida; she too had done a stint as a child actor. She seemed a little lost among her own cohort and I sometimes suspected she was having a rough adjustment, whether to New York or college life or the hothouse of the Pratt Writing Program, I wasn't sure. But I thought she'd be a good fit with Eli and his crew. Also, to be perfectly candid, I wanted to work with her again before I left. For all these reasons, I asked the director of the program to give her a spot in my spring elective, despite the fact that it was already full and had a wait list.

If it could go without saying that I saw something of myself in Eli, and that our teacher-student relationship and subsequent friendship were both, at some level, rooted in this sense of recognition, it probably needs to be said outright that the same was true of Anika. For obvious reasons, it is more difficult for a straight male professor to mentor a female student than a male one without certain questions being raised as to the nature of his interest. And yet, if the professor's response to this difficulty is to only mentor male students, he is depriving all those women of their chance to *be* mentored, to make a lasting connection with a writer in the generation above theirs. And not for nothing, he is also depriving himself of that same connection. To try to mold the minds of people whose minds you refuse to know seems to me an act of hubris, and bound to fail.

Eli's cohort all graduated in 2015—they left when I did—but Anika was still in her senior year when Eli died. As I said before, she is the person who called me with the news, and from that point forward we were in regular contact. It sounded like the whole Pratt Writing Program was, understandably, in a dark place. People were traumatized, lashing out, hurting one another and themselves. Rather than relieved to be removed from all this, I felt guilty about being far away while people I cared about were struggling to hang on.

I would not, under normal circumstances, have considered a friendship with a student while she was still a student, but these were not normal circumstances (and she was no longer my student). We emailed a lot, sometimes talked on the phone. She told me about the funeral, about spending time with Eli's parents, John and Dorothy, and about her own family. We talked about the things that families go through and the choices people make; what it means to love someone while still holding them accountable—in your own mind, if nowhere else—for the mistakes they made and what those mistakes have cost.

Honesty can accommodate anger but not resentment.

Love can be clear-eyed enough to include judgment but only if it also contains forgiveness.

In this way Anika improbably became the only person other than my wife, my sister, and a few close friends with whom I spoke about my father, during what turned out to be the last year of his life. As Amy Hempel puts it in "In the Cemetery Where Al Jolson Is Buried" (a story I had in fact taught to both Anika and to Eli when they were each freshmen), we became "fluent now in the language of grief."

I got off the C train at the Bedford–Nostrand stop, lugged my suitcase to the coffee shop near Pratt where we were meeting. We talked for about an hour. She gave me a crystal from her altar and a patch for Eli's band, Luxury Condos. The patch is a black fabric rectangle with white screen printing: the band's initials and a cracked martini glass whose stem is intersected by an arrow in flight. The band played hardcore punk and I'd always meant to make it to one of their shows but never had.

Back in Indiana, I took the patch and the crystal out of my backpack and tried to figure out what to do with them. I had a small wooden box that my mother had given me (it is carved to look like a book, the lid its front cover), which I had brought to hold my wallet and keys, only they hadn't fit, so I had been keeping change in it. I dumped the change out, put the patch and the crystal in. Feeling that this was correct, but somehow not enough, I added a spent shell that I'd kept from my trip to the shooting range, the first round I'd fired, the one that had bounced off my glasses and ended up in my shirt. This trio of objects in the small wooden box became my own little altar, so to speak. When I came home to Portland in May it came with me. When I left again in August, I left the bullet behind but put the patch and the crystal into a small pocket of my backpack, and that's where they've stayed ever since, except when I take them out to look at them. They're on my desk beside my notebook as I write these lines.

I never felt as far away from New York as on the day of Eli's funeral, which wasn't in New York anyway, but in Northampton, Massachusetts, where he'd grown up. I remember talking to my father about this, telling him how much I had liked

Eli, how much I'd admired him, as a writer and as a person. How in light of the sheer randomness and stupidity of what had happened, I was torn between two mutually exclusive feelings: that I had betrayed him by not doing something—*anything*—to somehow get between him and his addiction, and that he had somehow betrayed me by overdosing.

Dad listened to me for a long time. He let me get everything out. When I was finally finished, he reminded me that what had happened to Eli had nothing to do with me. He told me that it was just as delusional to take Eli's death as a personal affront as it was to imagine that I could have prevented it. The latter notion, he thought, was particularly pernicious, because it was at its heart a fantasy of my own self-importance, a version of *Only I can fix it*. "The fact is," Dad said, "people are complicated, and sometimes you can help them out and sometimes you can't. You can be there for them as much as they'll let you, but in the end people have to save themselves, and they either do or they don't."

Dad calmed me down and helped me get a handle on myself. He helped me recognize that what I actually felt was helpless. I wanted Eli's death to be a missing homework assignment, something he could make up for with a late-night cram session and some extra credit. I wanted to be his teacher again, to be able to say, "Listen, you had a bad week, but let's not let this wreck your final grade." Dad, of all people, was the one who had to tell me, "You feel helpless because you are helpless. You can pretend that that's not true or you can admit that it is, but it'll be just as true either way." It was some of the best advice he ever gave me. I have often wondered whether he knew that he was also telling me something about how to deal with him.

———

The letter of condolence to Eli's parents was one of the hardest things I've ever had to write, including the letter I sent my father in 2007 and the darkest parts of this book you are reading now. I put it off for days, for weeks, appalled and ashamed at my own silence but still unready to face up to what had happened, for it to be real and true. Eventually Eli's father, John, wrote to me. He said a lot of generous things about my role in Eli's life and what I had meant to Eli as a teacher. I sat at my desk and cried for a while, knowing that this was the moment when the ice around my heart and in my throat would melt. It would simply have to melt. And so it did.

I wrote back to John. I told him how talented his son had been. What it had meant to me to know him, first as a student and then as a writer and a friend. As I wrote, I realized that this was Eli's grad school rec letter, the one that had been forming itself in my mind for a couple of years now, waiting for the day it would be asked for. But instead of sending it to Iowa or Columbia, I was writing it as an inexcusably belated letter of condolence to his parents. A reply in a Gmail thread.

In the months after Eli's death, I learned a lot about where he came from, how he got to be as special as he was. More than I probably would have had occasion to learn had he lived. When I wanted to publish a second story of Eli's in *The*

Literary Review, John and Dorothy gave me their blessing. When Dad died they were among the first to send a note to me. Anika told me that John and Dorothy had been hosting groups of Eli's friends at the family home in Northampton; they'd invite everyone up for the weekend, or they'd come down to New York for a day and take them to dinner.

Eli's family was determined to make the best they could of the worst thing that had ever happened to them. And they insisted on remembering their son not as some hazy angel but rather as the unique and irreplaceable person he had actually been: promise, flaws, ambitions, mistakes, struggles; all of it. At every turn they tried to memorialize him in a way that he would have appreciated. They helped one of his friends establish a scholarship for aspiring writers at his old high school, and staged a weekend of performances and writing workshops in his name. They lovingly talked smack about his punk-rock vanities, his pretense of having grown up working-class. John is especially funny when ragging on the South Boston accent that Eli seems to have taught himself around the time he relocated to New York City, and that it took me three years to realize was bullshit. In this way they became my teachers. In those first hard months after I lost Dad, I looked to them as a model. I thought about their honesty and integrity and love and endurance and set it as the standard for myself.

The same week that I moved to Hattiesburg, in August 2017, I received a note from Eli's family, announcing that the unveiling of his headstone would take place on Sunday, September 10. I was stunned by this. Sometimes Eli's death felt as fresh as the front page of the morning paper. Other times it was hard to remember that there had ever been a time before his absence was a fact. I could not decide what I could not believe: that it had *nearly* been a year or that it had *not even* been a year. I tried to think back to last October: before Hattiesburg, before Indiana, before Dad's death, before Trump's election, before Eli's overdose. I thought of a line from *Jesus' Son* (Denis Johnson too was alive a year ago): "That world! These days it's all been erased and they've rolled it up like a scroll and put it away somewhere. Yes, I can touch it with my fingers. But where is it?"

As it happened, I was already scheduled to be in New York that weekend to participate in a writing conference. They were flying me up there, but all my obligations to the conference would be finished on Saturday. I made arrangements with Anika to drive to Northampton from Brooklyn together. I told John that I would be there.

Strong Theft in Northampton

The maggid of Mezritch said: "Every lock has its key which is fitted to it and opens it. But there are strong thieves who know how to open without keys. They break the lock. So every mystery in the world can be unriddled by that particular kind of meditation fitted to it. But God loves the thief who breaks the lock open: I mean the man who breaks his heart for God."

—MARTIN BUBER, *Tales of the Hasidim*

In June 1995 I was bar mitzvahed. I hated the whole bar mitzvah year. Hated dressing up, was scared of the boy-girl dances. Could not abide the emptiness of the ritual. This last sounds anachronistic, an adult's revisionist reading, but it isn't. After seven years of twice-a-week Hebrew school that was basically afternoon daycare, I thought *haftorah* study was where, finally, we were going to get into the good stuff. Instead, the cantor only wanted me to memorize by ear. He gave me a cassette tape of himself singing the portion and told me to follow along with the transliteration until I knew it by heart. The deepest conversation we ever had was about space aliens. I had come to my lesson wearing one of those oh-so-'90s T-shirts with a big alien head on it (glow-in-the-dark, natch). The cantor took note of my alien and asked if I thought such things could be real. He said that he hoped so, because something like that would be pretty cool. (Within two years I would be buying pot from his son.) I realized with a sinking heart that he was just some guy with a career, no more a man of God than my stockbroker father.

I was arguing with my parents about the bar mitzvah thing, and I got so angry I thought my head was going to explode. I was telling them I didn't want to go through with it and they were telling me I had to, and I did not know how to explain to them that the problem wasn't (as they believed) that I didn't take it seriously, but rather that it seemed to me nobody was taking it seriously enough. I ran out of the house and grabbed my bicycle and pedaled as hard as I could, though I didn't get very far. I didn't try to get far. I went to a friend's house, seeking something like sanctuary, assuming in my naïveté that another set of parents might be made to understand what mine had not.

By the time I got to my friend David's house I was a mess. David was the only Jewish kid I knew who wasn't in Hebrew school and wasn't having one of these gauche blowouts. (In fact, he was to be bar mitzvahed that summer at Mount Masada on a family trip to Israel, but I didn't see why that might make his parents anything other than my natural allies here.) I remember knocking on their door and the house-keeper telling me, in Spanish, that David wasn't home. But I spent a lot of time at that house and she knew me, and she could see I was upset. David's parents found me in their kitchen: hyperventilating, twelve years old, trying to explain to them that I didn't want to be Jewish and didn't think it was fair that I had to be. I don't know now whether the disgust on David's father's face was real or whether I'm imagining it, but I can see it clear as anything.

When I was calm enough, David's mother made me call my parents. My father was either too angry to get on the phone or too angry for my mother to let him near it, so she took the call, expressed her mortification at the scene I'd caused and the things she assumed (rightly) that I had said. I'd been gone from the house for less than an hour, traveled approximately a mile. Did I need to be picked up or would I come home on my own? That was her only question. I would come home, I told her. And I did.

Here, in his own words, is my father's explanation of why I must be bar mitzvahed.

"It doesn't matter what you believe or don't believe. You do it because of who else has done it before you, who else is doing it now, and who else will do it in the future. You do it to be with them because you are them and they are you, whether you like it or not."

At the time, this only confirmed my darkest suspicions about the hollowness of the traditions, the faithlessness of the faith. But curiously, it was enough to get me to cease rebellion. Call it Jewish guilt or just being outnumbered: I wasn't going to take on all those people. *All of us, past, present, future, and you can't do this one thing which anyway is throw you a party?* Well, when you put it like that.

Dad also stressed to me over and over how important the bar mitzvah was to my mother. I held this against her, in a low-grade way, for years, until I was old enough to figure out that she probably couldn't have cared less one way or the other, that all things being equal she almost certainly would have rather been spared the headache and the expense. It was always Dad who wanted it, but characteristically he could not own that desire, that need. Only someone else's needs (real or projected) were a good enough reason for any given thing to actually happen.

So I had the bar mitzvah. My *haftorah* portion was Naso, from Judges, which tells the story of Samson. I memorized the Hebrew phonetically and learned the cantillation from the cantor's recording. On the day of the ceremony I would chant my portion before the congregation, and then deliver a speech—in English—analyzing its lessons.

In the months leading up to the bar mitzvah service, Dad and I sat at the kitchen table for hours, night after night, going over the Samson story, forming opinions and generating ideas, which he took down on a yellow legal pad. He typed up the notes and I shaped them into a rough draft, which I then printed and read aloud to him. We both made notes on the hard copy for further adjustments to word choice and style. (He was teaching me how to edit and revise: The process I've just described is essentially the same one that I still use today.)

I have copies of two of our interim drafts and so can see just how closely we worked, as well as what our process was like. A sentence describing Samson's "superhuman strength and abilities" appears in the earlier draft, but is cut from the later draft because the description is rendered redundant by a change we've made elsewhere in the text. The sentence "This led to a bet and a riddle with the Philistines at his wedding feast" is revised to read "a riddle and a bet" instead. This construction distributes the short "e" sounds of "led," "bet," and "wedding" more evenly throughout the sentence, adding a bit of music and making the whole thing flow more smoothly.

Ours was a revisionist reading of the Samson story. We argued—provocatively, in the context—that this great Jewish hero was not a hero at all, but rather "a classic, flawed, failed, tragic figure," whose "fall from grace, his slide down the ladder from great beautiful protector to pathetic spectacle was predictable if not inevitable. [. . .] Had he better used his power and managed his life, the benefits to him and the Jewish people could have been much larger."

The speech took more than ten minutes to deliver, which if you're wondering is way too long for this sort of thing. But I was a strong performer and we had rehearsed it down to every stress and pause and punch line. I gave the speech to an audience of several hundred people, and when it was over I received a standing ovation, which is all but unheard-of in a conservative synagogue on Shabbat morning. The rabbi, who'd had reservations about the speech and almost refused to approve it, was floored. He said he'd never seen anything like that reaction in all his years.

Because I'd agreed to fulfill the obligations of the bar mitzvah service, Dad said that the reception could be as goofy and irreverent as I liked. Most of my friends' bar mitzvahs had been formal affairs, black tie optional on a Saturday night. Mine was jeans casual at a beach-themed nightclub that we'd rented out for the afternoon. There were video games and sumo-suit wrestling, some kind of human gyroscope thing you climbed inside to get spun around. The invitation itself had been full of jokes, which Dad and I wrote together. Directions to the venue started with Earth's position in the solar system. The souvenir T-shirt (there's always a souvenir T-shirt; don't ask me why) depicted a lizard riding a surfboard.

My memories of the party are a blur of aunts, uncles, cousins, grandparents, great-grandparents; all my friends and my parents' friends. And how happy Dad was. He loved my bar mitzvah. He remembered every single thing that happened that day and loved to relive it. He'd tell the story, get this wistful, proud tone in his voice. What I said before, about how unheard-of a standing ovation was and how shocked and impressed the rabbi was—that's all him talking. He told me that stuff so many times, my own narrative of the day owes less to my firsthand experience of it than it does to his, the story that he turned it into and what that story meant to him. So forget for a second what the bar mitzvah did or didn't or does or doesn't mean to me. It was one of the best days of my father's life.

———

They baffle and incense you, the old masters of fringe Judaism, those riddling rabbis. The maggid of Mezritch chooses theft and heartbreak as his metaphors, then finds in them the locus of God's love. There is no assimilating this wisdom, no taming it. And they would not wish to see it tamed because they knew that God is wild. I don't mean that wildness is an attribute, a character trait, of His, though there's ample enough evidence in the Torah for that as well. *Ehyeh asher ehyeh,* God tells Moses: *I am that I am,* though the Hebrew also allows for a less reflexive translation: *I am that I shall be.* In either case it is clear that His immanence is inherent in His presence.

God is the wild, or He is wildness itself. Everything unknown and overmastering: the stifling dark desert as well as the pillar of fire we follow through it, if we do follow. Kabbalists and tzadiks and hasidim and maggids; they speak in parables that do not resolve to lessons. Though their tales take the form of stories and often offer something like an epiphanic moment, they are closer to koans than to fables. They only ever suggest definitive answers by way of teasing, and even if a given tale achieves something like lucidity or conclusiveness, it will be contradicted by the next story told. These guys knew better than to offer answers. They knew that there are no such things as answers—not to life, not to death, not to God—and this unanswerability is, at bottom, the truest lesson, the only lesson, that they have to teach. A mystery is only ever unriddled after it's over. The only answer to life is more life and the only answer to a story is another story.

Northampton, Massachusetts, is, optimistically, three hours from New York. Anika had borrowed her boyfriend's Toyota 4Runner. She picked me up from my friend Robin's apartment at 8 A.M. on Sunday, September 10, 2018. In the car with her was another former student, Madison, who had been in Anika's cohort at Pratt, and a couple of their other friends whom I'd never met before.

It was a long day, a hard day, but it was also a good day. We shouldn't hesitate to say that. There were at least a hundred people gathered around the grave. The stone was shrouded in a cream-colored sheet. The ceremony was brief. The rabbi explained that there's actually very little in the way of specifics about what to *do* at an unveiling; it's basically a folk tradition that over the eons has become mainstream.

Jews don't think much about the afterlife. It isn't where we focus our faith. Nevertheless, we do have a concept of judgment and of the eternal, which is reflected in much of our liturgy and prayers. We believe that the soul is judged by God twelve months after the body dies. It is for this reason that the headstone is unveiled in the eleventh month after death, so that mourning concludes before judgment is rendered. This is understood as an expression of our faith in the justice of whatever judgment God may pass, but also of our faith that the departed will be judged righteous. If we mourned through the twelfth month, this would be an expression of doubt in the Creator's wisdom, and perhaps, too, a form of campaigning for divine clemency, which would itself be an expression of doubt in the integrity of the one who was lost. This was why my friend Joshua had said *Baruch dayan ehmet* to me when I told him that Dad had died.

Blessed is the true judge.

I'm talking about all this like I'm some expert, but all that I am telling you I learned that day. That perfect New England autumn day, 72 degrees and cloudless, the bluest sky anyone could ask for, the small cemetery nestled among tall trees, mourners standing elbow to elbow, to be as near to one another as we could be, determined to translate our sorrow into remembrance and celebration.

After the unveiling, everyone was invited to a new community arts center that Dorothy had spent the last several years working to get built. We ate and drank and had an open mic in a bright, spacious room in the basement (a room that, a year later, would be named for Eli). Eli's family read from his writing. His friends from home told stories about growing up, getting into trouble, about how Eli's house was always the place you could go, where there was no limit to the number of kids who were welcome to stay for dinner, to sleep over, to hang out. His friends from Pratt read poems they'd written for him;

there were inside jokes and a few cryptic allusions, and I had the sense that amid all the public tributes something more private was occurring: It wasn't just Eli they were laying to rest, but also whatever had happened in the chaos around his death, the hole that had been gouged into the center of these kids' collective life. You could feel the broken threads beginning to knit back together. Or I thought that I could, though it really wasn't my business, and so, not knowing precisely *what* was happening, I tried to let it be enough *that* it was happening—and to leave it to those to whom it belonged. I read the parable of the Strong Thief, the same text that stands as the epigraph to this chapter, which I had handy because the first time I'd encountered it, years earlier, I'd saved a copy of it on my phone and have kept it with me ever since. (I suppose if I were the kind of person who made altars, I would print it out on a card and place it by the crystal and the patch.)

When the reception was over, Eli's parents invited everyone back to their home. Most folks said their goodbyes at that point, but a bunch of us continued on to the house. There we spent the afternoon drinking wine first and coffee later, heating up leftovers, talking and telling stories, filling the day with life.

The older I get, the less concerned I am about the specifics of what a given believer believes—still less with the rigidity of the dogma. What interests me is the condition under which belief itself becomes possible. I crave the inner space that faith pries open, even if—perhaps especially if—that space is empty and even if it closes up again. The strong thief breaks the lock, but he does not get to live in the house he enters; he only gets to keep what he can carry with him when he runs away.

In *My Bright Abyss,* his book of essays on faith and illness, Christian Wiman quotes Simone Weil: "We must believe in God in every way, except that he does not exist, for we have not reached the point where he might exist." Wiman extrapolates: "Contemporary people . . . tend to be obsessed by *whether* God exists. What Weil is saying is that this is not beside the point exactly, but a misdirection: God exists apart from our notions of what it means to exist, and there is a sense in which our most pressing existential question has to be outgrown before it can be answered."

Faith is the form of that outgrowing. It is our willingness to shed the question like old skin, and dwell instead in readiness and possibility. Belief is that possibility realized, our readiness called upon, but it is not scored like a home run or handed down like a prison sentence. What I mean is that it is not final, not static. It will be achieved and lost many times over, like grief or ecstasy, and each experience will leave its mark, and shape the next one, just as Jacob's proof of having wrestled with the angel was that when he walked away with his blessing—the blessing of Israel—he was limping on his hip.

In the words of Christ in John 12:36, "While ye have the light, believe in the light, that ye may be the children of light." Or, as the Grateful Dead put it in "Ripple," "Reach out your hand if your cup be empty / If your cup is full may it be again."

The strong thief breaks the lock.

The lock is the silence broken by the song.

I stand at Eli's grave and listen as the rabbi leads us through a recitation of the Mourner's Kaddish, and then the singing of "Ohseh Shalom," which is nothing more than the last lines of the Kaddish set to a tune and incanted over and over.

> *Ohseh shalom bimromav*
> *hoo ya'ah-seh shalom aleynu*
> *v'al kol Yisrael, ve'imru amen.*

I hear the unified rising of the voices, all of us singing, and I realize that I hear myself among that chorus, that my lips and my throat know the melody and the ancient words.

You do it because of who else has done it before you, who else is doing it now, and who else will do it in the future. You do it to be with them, because you are them and they are you.

For twenty years and more I have been unable or unwilling to understand this. But as I stand in the cemetery and hear my own voice singing, I finally know what my father meant, and know, too, that he was right. I weep for him and for Eli and for myself as well. We sing to mourn and to declare the end of mourning, and when the song is over there is nothing for us to do but embrace each other and dry our tears. To timidly inquire about directions to the arts center. I put my arm around Anika's shoulders. She hands me her car keys. We walk together away from the grave and into the living mystery of an autumn afternoon.

Two Trips to Sunrise

I took two trips to Sunrise, Florida, in the spring of 2017. I was met there both times by my wife and my sister. The first trip was in February, a few weeks after the phone call when Dad described falling down in his bedroom and getting stuck on the floor. The second trip was in April and felt uncannily like a "revision" of the first trip, involving all the same people and apartments and five o'clock suppers at bad chain restaurants. Only Dad himself was missing, having been revised out of the story. And our task that weekend was, in a sense, editorial: to separate the keepsakes and heirlooms from the clutter and junk, get the apartment ready to sell.

I have never been able to untangle these two visits in my mind. Every time I tried to write about them individually they bled into each other, wanting to be told at once. And this second encounter with the Stuff got me thinking about the first time I'd sorted through it all, that day in Nashville a few years earlier. I began to revisit some of the assertions I'd made at that time about what it means to mourn for someone while they are still alive. How did my thoughts about grief hold up now that they were no longer hypotheticals? How did I feel about what I'd said about losing my father, in the harsh light of now having actually lost him?

When I described going through the Stuff the first time, I mentioned finding a poem that Dad had written. I said that as far as I knew, he never wrote another. This is no longer true.

I don't find a lot of poems, but I do find some. They are written longhand on legal pads or on loose leaf; one is in a draft email, no recipient in the To box. Like the one I found in Nashville, these are in stumbling AA/BB, the rhymes as stiff as a third grader's, and any poem that runs longer than a page is unfinished. Dad never read poetry, or imaginative literature of any kind, unless you count mysteries; he liked to try to solve the crimes before the detectives, and he usually did. There were always plenty of books in the house growing up, and I was always encouraged both to read and to write, but when I think back on it now I realize that all the works of literary fiction—from *The Lord of the Rings* to *Watership Down*— were Mom's books.

When, at age ten, I discovered Stephen King, it was Dad who stood up for my right to read what many considered too graphic, vulgar, and scary. "If he's smart enough to read it, he's allowed to read it" was Dad's verdict—delivered to every elementary and middle school teacher I ever had, who each in their turn confiscated a King book from me and called my parents to ask if they knew what I was reading. "Justin is eleven years old," he sneered at Mrs. McClain. "Where do you think he got the money to buy that book? How do you think that he got to the store?" But it was Mom who read those books along with me, sometimes before I read them and sometimes after, in case I had questions about the things that I was exposed to in their pages. It was exactly the sort of parental duty that Dad, under usual circumstances, would have reserved for himself. It's obvious in retrospect that he must have let Mom do it because he knew all the ghost cars and zombie cats and demon clowns would have bored him clear out of his mind.

I'm certain that my father never shared the poems he wrote. He probably never told anyone that they existed, and he certainly didn't mention them to his son, the writer. The poems seem to have been written almost involuntarily, at moments of such deep despair that he simply did not know what else to do.

In *My Bright Abyss,* Christian Wiman writes, "Poetry has its uses for despair. It can carve a shape for pain; it can give one's loss a form and dimension that it might *be* loss and not simply a hopeless haunting." In *The Poet's Art,* the critic M. L. Rosenthal makes a similar point, describing poetry as "the art that uses language to delight the heart or break it but also to open it to itself." But confessional writing only becomes poetry, Rosenthal argues, when the writer is able to see the work as a body of raw material separate from himself, and can begin to shape it. The work must then develop its own intelligence, a capacity for induction that the artist instigates but cannot fully control. Art becomes art when it is capable of speaking back to the artist, of originating emotions, ideas, and meanings that have previously gone unacknowledged or did not exist until the work coaxed them into being. Art is the art of self-surprise.

With no disrespect to Dad intended, I believe that this is why the longer poems remain unfinished. He wrote poems when he felt the urgent need to rid himself of something and could find no other place to put it. In each case, he stopped as soon as the urgency subsided, or else at the moment that the inductive turn might have occurred. He did not allow the poems to speak back to him because he did not want to hear what they would have said.

Among his papers I find a document from US bankruptcy court, dated 5/8/1997, confirming discharge of all debts. It was a week before his forty-fifth birthday, the same week that he wrote what I'd previously thought was his only poem. So this then was the crisis. Okay. I now also know that he offered Mom a divorce at the time, and that she got as far as consulting with a family friend about the logistics of taking such a step, but that in the end she decided to stay with him. She figured they'd get through it, she told me. She wasn't ready to give up on them or him.

This also means that when Dad confronted me about smoking pot, and I'd thought he was going to give me the

Divorce Talk, I wasn't that far off. The prospect had been seriously discussed only a few months earlier.

My father's parents hit him up for cash in 1997, around the same time he was declaring bankruptcy. I don't know how much they asked for or why they needed it, but I know it was the first time he turned them down. And I'm sure that he wanted to help, that he wished he could, but the money simply didn't exist. They regarded this as high treason and were so angry that they hardly spoke to him or saw their grandchildren for the next seven years. They had never been as present in my and my sister's lives as our maternal grandparents, but after this episode they basically disappeared. My sister has no memories of them between when she was nine and sixteen years old. A tepid attempt at reconnection was made in 2004, because of the impending move to Tennessee. They didn't come over to the house, so my sister and I never saw or spoke to them, but they did call Dad to say goodbye.

What all this means is that it was in a sense incorrect to locate the origin of Dad's decline in 2007, as I did near the beginning of this book, when I said I was trying to "tell . . . but also to deconstruct" the story of his last ten years. The tempting neatness of the ten-year span elides the ten years that preceded it, both in my telling of Dad's story and, crucially, in his own telling of it. One could just as easily have started with the bankruptcy declaration in 1997, which is what first sent my mother onto the job market after ten years running a small business.

It had started at our dining-room table: using her art and design skills to hand-paint kids' names onto rocking chairs, coat hangers, and piggy banks; batches of personalized favors for birthday parties. She sold directly to friends and gave samples to local stores that would then take custom orders, which Mom would fill. Over time, the product line grew and she developed a knack for noticing emerging trends, for sensing what would sell. With a friend who was also selling hand-decorated gifts made at home, she opened The Name Game, a store where they sold what they made alongside scented candles, jewelry boxes, and Beanie Babies at the height of the craze. They invested in a high-end printer and began to design and print wedding and bar mitzvah invitations. Soon they had a couple of part-time employees and a healthy clientele, but the store only ever made enough money to pay for itself, and by 1997 that wasn't going to cut it anymore.

She got a job with one of the companies that had supplied The Name Game with products. The position was for a product development buyer, and she knew how to buy and what would sell from having run the store. It was her first corporate job, at forty-one years old and with no BA, but she excelled at the work and this led, in due course, to the job that took them to Nashville, where everything fell apart.

Mom had been with Dad since she was a teenager. The unpredictability of his manias, the intensity of his rages, the depths of his depressions were all things she'd long accustomed herself to living with. It would not have occurred to her to question them, or to leave him on account of them. If they'd all moved together, like she had wanted to do, maybe they would have stayed married until he died. What she failed to understand about herself during the year she spent alone in Tennessee was how the aloneness was changing her. The time apart from Dad put the worst aspects of his character into a sharper relief than she'd ever seen them before. And it must be said that he was at his worst, his cruelest and most volatile and unreasonable, those first years in Nashville. My mother must have been the one to realize, sometime in 2005 or 2006, that the marriage had already ended, that it had ended years earlier, on the day that she left Florida alone.

This version of the story, then, doesn't begin in 2007; it ends there.

But the 1997 story is no origin story either. My parents were never spendthrifts; they weren't addicts or drunks. The road to bankruptcy must have been long, fitful, and slow. How did they get there? To answer that question I guess we should go back *another* decade, to 1987, when Dad would have been thirty-five, the age that I am now as I sit here writing this. He would have been in the first year of his job as a stockbroker at Corporate Securities Group, the job he would hold longer than any other, and Mom would have been thirty-one. I was starting kindergarten; my sister was hardly a gleam in the eye—

Stop.

Earlier, when I wrote about my frustration with Dad's attachment to the Stuff, and how annoyed I was at having had to travel to Nashville and sort through it while he yelled at me on the phone, I described "trying to get permission to throw away as much of his precious garbage as I possibly could."

I feel bad about having written this, which is not to say

that I now think I was wrong. Dad was a pack rat, and there's no denying that a lot of the Stuff (both the forty-box version I took out of the storage unit and the twenty-box version that got shipped to Florida) were items of no financial, sentimental, historical, or practical value to anybody, including him. Forget whether they should have been thrown out when he sold the Nashville house or whether they should have been shipped down to Florida in 2015; the real question is whether they should have gone to Nashville when they sold the Miami house in 2004. The answer, for the most part, is no.

And yet I feel bad. Because it's clear to me now, in a way that it wasn't then, that if I disregard the question of the relative value of the Stuff, and treat its existence as a given, it is easy to understand why Dad wanted it. This was everything he owned in the world, and whatever meager hope he allowed himself of living something like a normal life again was based on two inextricable ideas: getting his things back, and having somewhere to put them. A home. As grateful as he was that Michael had stepped up and bought him an apartment, he was angry—and vocally so—about the fact that the budget would only allow for a small one-bedroom. He campaigned hard for a two- or three-bedroom, solely because he wanted to be able to host his children when we visited. He hated that there was no longer a family home to which we could return. And I suppose it bears stating again that the fact that such a place did not exist was due entirely to his own self-destructive instincts and financial mismanagement. But really, so what? He knew that as well as anyone, and nobody had a harder time living with it than he did.

There's another reason that I feel bad about what I wrote.

My life has, at least so far, not unfolded very much like my father's, but there have been some key ways in which our experiences have resonated. The dislocation I felt and the depression I dealt with in the first year that I spent in Portland were remarkably similar to what he went through after relocating to Nashville, and again after moving into the hotel. I'd like to think I rose to the occasions better than he did: by being willing to see a therapist, for example, or just by working through it and moving on. Still, it was hard, especially when these issues were compounded by the emotional and practical ramifications of being unemployed.

If I had been thirty years older . . .

If I'd already been out of work for nearly a decade . . .

If I hadn't had my writing to sustain me . . .

Would I have fared any better than Dad did?

When I did find work, it was far-flung: Indiana, Mississippi. Don't get me wrong: I was honored to be offered these jobs, desperate for the money, and grateful for the time to write. I enjoyed getting to know these cities and regions, coming to understand them in their granularity and contradiction, their messiness and potential. But I didn't plan to spend nearly two out of the first three years of my marriage living on the other side of the country from my wife. I did not anticipate the psychic damage that would accrue from living what was, in spirit if not quite letter, a hotel life: an empty bed in an unfamiliar city, a borrowed IKEA desk, pasta for one.

This, too, is similar to what Dad went through during those years in the extended-stay hotel, then at his parents' apartment, and finally in Sunrise Lakes. A place he could call his own, but only sort of. It had come furnished with the previous occupant's couch and bed and lounge chairs, her cramped dining table and ugly brown carpet and chintzy low-hanging chandelier. And of course he didn't own the apartment. He knew that he would never be kicked out of it, but it wasn't his. He had security but not self-determination. I can see why, in that context, getting the Stuff back was not a matter of stubbornness or pettiness—though it was certainly those things too—but rather something truly meaningful. It was, quite literally, all he had left in the world. Maybe, I sometimes think to myself, something conspired to send me into my own exile to grant me insight into what my father endured in his.

The last time I saw my father alive was about a month before he died, and about a month after he told me that awful story about falling down and getting stuck between his bed and his desk. Amanda, Melanie, and I met up in Florida for a long weekend, February 17–21. On the last day of the trip, we went in with an agenda. First, we wanted to get Dad signed up for Medicare ahead of his sixty-fifth birthday (May 15), at which point he could begin to receive it; second, we wanted him to eat more fresh and nutritious food.

We stopped at a Publix grocery store on the way to his house. Since we couldn't force him to buy healthier food, we decided to cook it for him ourselves. Amanda had a recipe for veggie baked ziti and Melanie had one for some kind of granola protein muffin, a high-calorie health bomb. We bought everything we'd need at the Publix, including kitchen supplies, since we didn't know what he would have to cook with but assumed that it wouldn't be much. We bought snacks and fruit. We knew that we had to just show up with it all, not present it as an option, because if given the chance he would refuse us: too much money, too much fuss.

Amanda and Melanie cooked—more cooking than that apartment had seen since he'd lived there—and I kept Dad busy by getting him talking. *How's the writing going? How are classes? What's Indiana like? You believe what Trump just said?*

It was cool enough outside that we convinced him to open the windows and the sliding glass door, shut the A/C off, let some fresh air in. We even got him to turn off the TV.

The ziti was portioned into single-serving plastic containers and then frozen. Melanie, the lawyer, helped Dad parse the Medicare paperwork. They made some calls, got everything ready. We ordered dinner from a Thai place, and Amanda and I picked it up, brought it back to the apartment. Plenty of leftovers.

As I often find is the case when I'm writing about my father, when I'm remembering him and times we spent together, I find myself recalling less content than form. Proximity, duration, intimacy. Not what we talked about but that we talked. We were parenting him a bit and he was letting us. It seemed, for the first time in years, like progress was possible. That there were things for us and for him to look forward to. I remember that Dad was happy. Thrilled, in fact. That he got to see his kids, spend time with his daughter-in-law, have a houseful of people like in the old days.

It was well past dark by the time we left his apartment; we all had crack-of-dawn flights in the morning: Amanda back to Portland, Melanie to New York, me to Indianapolis. Dad, for his part, was nodding off on the couch. He'd had more stimulation that day than he usually got in a week, his belly was full of food, and his medicine was working. He was always so exhausted from the shaking, and from the constant pacing with which he tried to mitigate the shaking, that as soon as his medicine kicked in he usually fell asleep. Sixty minutes, maybe ninety—two hours would be a miracle. If it had not been the last night of our trip we would have left without waking him. But we could not leave without saying goodbye.

He gave us each a long hug and said thank you. I told him that we'd do it again soon.

Heading back to the hotel, we were tired but buzzing with happiness. The day had gone so much better than we had dared to hope it would. Our strategy had worked! This then was going to be the new model: coordinated effort, a united front, a focus on tangible outcomes over philosophical questions, just enough imperial affect to keep things moving along. When Medicare kicked in, we'd find him a new doctor. We'd get him back in the habit of eating real food.

Earlier I wrote, "I grieve two years for my father and when it is over I lay his ghost to rest, release myself." This sentence is both true and not true. When I wrote it, I did not yet know what grief was, or not completely. I still don't, maybe never will. Maybe nobody does. Mourning is, among other things, a form of preservation, and so in a sense it is never over and never should be. The hubris—the error—in the line as I wrote it is less in the presumption of knowing grief than in the presumption of having known it fully.

And in having presumed that the work of it was finished.

Or that it ever would be.

Death revises life. The way a life ends rewrites the story, not only *what* it means but *how* it means. The life is rewritten, first and foremost, as the path to that death. In our father's case, my and my sister's worst fear came true: Our father died alone and nobody even knew.

The temptation is strong to read his whole life as a long tailspin toward this oblivion. At times—at the worst times—such a reading is irresistible. But to read his life through the lens of his death is to ignore the ferocity with which he struggled against damning odds to live something like a normal life, a good life. To be a loving father and husband. And it ignores the many ways in which he succeeded. His biggest and dearest-held dreams were not for himself but for his children, and in his children his dreams came true.

My sister is the hotshot lawyer that everyone always told him he could have been, and that he sometimes talked regretfully about not having tried to become. And me, well, I'm the repressed artist part of him, brought to life and let loose. I think of all the school projects and class speeches he helped me write, the rock band he fronted for a hot minute all those ages ago, the hundreds of black-and-white photographs he took in the only art class he allowed himself as an undergraduate. Printed on card stock and mounted on foam board and saved for forty years. I saw them in Tennessee when I sorted all the Stuff in 2015, and I saw them again in South Florida when my dark prophecy ("Doing all the things I would do if he had died, and knowing that eventually I'll do it all again . . .") came true, so much sooner than I'd thought it would.

The only thing I was wrong about was that I'd imagined myself doing it alone.

Melanie and Amanda were there with me. We sat and looked together, going slowly, lingering lovingly as we made our stacks and piles. But still, gradually, making them: keep, toss, donate, toss, toss, donate, keep.

We found a packet of letters from Mom to him, from when they were apart while she was in New York. For a minute we were giddily reading them, cracking ourselves up at their cheesiness, but also reveling in the evidence of an era when they had been young and madly in love with each other and life was a big chance that they couldn't wait to take. We had to cut ourselves off when one letter got racy. My sister was particularly grossed out by a line where Mom, eighteen or nineteen years old at the time, tells Dad he is her "father, brother, lover" all in one. My sister did not know that this was less Freudian-pervy than hippie-dippy. Mom is paraphrasing the song "Together Alone" by Melanie Safka. A few years after this letter was written, that song would be played at their wedding as they walked down the aisle. Eleven years after that, in 1988, Mom and Dad would give me a sister and name her Melanie and buy a little house in North Miami Beach for us to live in.

His record collection, those four boxes of vinyl, were exactly as I'd found them in the storage unit in Nashville. As predicted, they had not been opened since they'd been shipped to Florida. I opened them now. I texted Mom and told her we were trying to find someone interested in buying the whole collection. They'd be worth more if we sold them individually, say on eBay, but not if I first had to pay to ship them to myself in Portland. I'd asked my aunts if they had any interest in taking on that project but it was more than they could handle. I was going to make an inventory, choose a few for keepsakes, and then start calling around to record stores.

For the first time in all our discussions of the Stuff, Mom said something that should have been obvious from the get-go but had never occurred to me before that moment. In fact it floored me. She said that they were her records too and that she would like to have them. My sister and I went to the UPS store. I taped the boxes shut without taking anything for myself, and we shipped them back to Tennessee, where I am happy to report that they are being played again. Mom bought a record player. When I visit she asks me if there's anything I want to hear.

Whenever I used to hear people say of someone who succumbed after a long battle with illness, "At least he's at peace now," I thought they were speaking metaphorically. I thought, too, that they were full of shit. I understand now that I was wrong on both counts.

My father's pain, both physical and psychic, had weight and volume. It was a permanent presence in his life and the lives of the people who knew him. It expanded and contracted. It was flammable, toxic, volatile. The silence since he has been gone is unimaginable. It terrifies and unsettles, but also—I won't mince words here—exhilarates and relieves. Every worried thought about how he's doing, every anxiety about his future (what will he need? how will we pay for it? what will the next phase of the nightmare be?), every strategy for managing him, every effort to fend off or mitigate disaster, every fear I ever had on his behalf: It's *all* silence now. There is so much open space in my mind, heart, and soul that I can hardly survey it, much less occupy it. I will spend the rest of my own life crossing that great plain.

Stereo up, windows down.

I am not saying I am glad he's gone. I am saying that I feel the absence of his suffering just as palpably as, for so long, I felt its presence. A storm has passed and a calm prevails: the "peace" of the apt platitude. That peace is here because he isn't here and yet it is also his, is him.

I'm never going to be one of those people who pushes a silver-lining-of-illness narrative, who asserts that it was all serving some ultimate purpose, some greater good, or—worst of all—"part of God's plan." No God of mine would have planned this. My father lived his whole life in turmoil, and his last years in constant, all-consuming pain. His illness took his health, his self-sufficiency, his intellect, and finally it took his life. He didn't deserve any of that. Nobody does. But this is a realm of experience in which the term "deserve" does not apply. I would give anything for him to have been spared what he suffered, and for my sister and me to have been spared having to watch it unfold, inexorable and nonsensical as biology or fate.

But here is a fact: My father's illness forced me to understand that the man who raised me, the man I was so angry at—whose shortcomings, misjudgments, and failures, both real and imagined, I wanted to reckon with and indict him for—no longer existed. He was replaced by a weaker man, one who would have been obliterated by the force of my anger if I had unleashed it. All this new man needed from me was love, patience, compassion, and sometimes a Target gift card. I know that I did not always rise to these occasions. That could probably go without saying but I will say it anyway. I need to say it. I wasn't always there for my father; I didn't always have what he needed, and sometimes I had it but didn't give it. I wasn't good enough. I'll carry that with me. But sometimes—maybe, by the end, most of the time—I was able to give him what he needed. That he allowed himself to receive it was its own kind of miracle. I'd like to think that this succor and repair—this redemption—could have happened if he'd stayed healthy, but I'd be lying if I said I was sure it would have. So while I will never say that I am "thankful" for his illness, I will say that I am thankful that we were granted a second chance, to love each other without reservation, to say and mean all of those things you usually only wish, after it's too late, that you had found the words to say.

We are standing in the open-air hallway outside of his apartment, saying our goodbyes. He's still a little foggy from having just been woken up. I can feel him in my arms, the fabric of his white polo shirt tucked into jeans that sit loose despite the belt being on its innermost notch. I can smell him, the animal fact of his presence, something I have never not known. His thinning hair half gray, grown out long enough to tuck behind his ears. He is skin and bone in my arms, shaking not from his illness now but from the love shuddering through him, crying for happiness for a change.

I make him promise to go back to sleep when we are gone. He says he will, but first he is going to see us off. He stands at the rail and watches us cross the parking lot, pile into the rental car. I'm driving. I reverse out of the spot, wave once, put the car into drive. I see him in the rearview mirror, a dark shape framed by the light of his open front door. He makes no move to go back inside and I know that he won't. Not until we are fully out of sight. And then, if I know him—and I do; I know him better than I have ever known another person—he will stand there awhile longer, not yet ready to let the day we've shared be over, to let the present become the past.

The Road Home

The days go slow but the weeks go fast. It's been eight months of driving Dad's car around Hattiesburg: to campus, the gym, the hip brewery downtown, the famous BBQ place out on Highway 98. And farther afield, all over Mississippi: to Oxford, Jackson, Taylor, and Water Town. To Pass Christian (I asked a colleague why it is pronounced "pass kristy-anne." "Is it French?" I said. "It's Mississippi," he replied) and Gulfport and Greenwood and Richton, because I had to see with my own eyes the former Emery Home for Unwed Mothers (now a private residence) where the poet Frank Stanford was born. And farther still, across the South: Sewanee, Nashville, Memphis, Tuscaloosa, Pensacola, New Orleans.

How many times, in these eight months, have I listened to *Beggars Banquet* by the Rolling Stones? A hundred? Two hundred? I know it by heart now, from the still thrillingly sinister opening notes of "Sympathy for the Devil" through the country-fried sketch comedy of "Dear Doctor" and the louche daydreams of "Jig-Saw Puzzle" on through "Street Fighting Man" (Dad's favorite) and the insanely problematic "Stray Cat Blues" ("I can see that you're fifteen years old . . .") which gets cringier every time I hear it but I never skip it because a rule is a rule, and the rule in this car is that when *Beggars Banquet* comes on it always plays uninterrupted, all the way to "Salt of the Earth," which can feel stirring or obnoxious depending on how much sarcasm and sneer you want to let yourself hear in Mick's delivery.

Before I know it, it is March again. Dad has been gone a year and it's time for me to start getting ready to leave. I'm bringing Dad's car back to Portland—or it's bringing me back—and we've decided to make a road trip out of the drive. Amanda's going to fly to New Orleans, where I'll meet her, then we'll camp and hike in national parks as we make our way. She's been plotting a route for us, reserving campsites, buying gear. She's been going on practice hikes in and around Portland: the gorge, the coast. What have I been doing? Dragging myself to the gym for an hour a few times a week, spending half of that time on weight machines and half on the elliptical. Listening to a lot of podcasts. Eating homemade salads alongside take-out Mexican food. Convincing myself that all this, somehow, constitutes getting in shape.

But I've got another trip to take before that one.

I've been invited by one of my undergrad writing professors from the University of Florida to visit the school's MFA program in my capacity as fiction editor of *The Literary*

Review. I'll talk about the magazine, sit on a panel with some other publishing people, give manuscript critiques to the grad students. They offered to fly me in, but it's only eight hours from Hattiesburg to Gainesville, and so it comes to pass that on the one-year anniversary of my father's death, I find myself driving his car and blasting his music as I take the same exit for campus that he and my mom took when they drove me here eighteen years ago, only I'm coming from the opposite direction. The last time I was in this town, in 2014, Dad was with me and he was driving. This same CD was probably on.

The school booked me a room at a brand-new hotel at the corner of Thirteenth Street and University Avenue, which in my day had been a tiny strip mall with a burrito place staffed by stoners from whom you could often beg buckets of unsold black beans at closing time. In my sister's years here, just before and after the '08 crash, it had been an empty field— the strip mall razed to make way for a new development that had never come. Only now it had.

I valeted the car, checked in, dropped my bags at the room, hit the street. I walked downtown, taking note along the way of what had survived and what had not. Gyro Plus and Leonardo's Pizza were both still there (though someone told me later that Leo's had lost their lease and was living on borrowed time). The Mellow Mushroom, where I'd worked, was long gone. The Top, in its day a punk-run vegan-friendly dive bar, had taken over its whole block and metamorphosed into some kind of family gastropub. The queer feminist bookstore was gone, but an indie upstart had opened a few blocks away.

I walked back toward the hotel but kept walking past it, into the so-called student ghetto, where blocks and blocks of houses had been torn down and replaced with apartment buildings. It felt like walking through a Disney Village. But old Abraham itself still stood, and from the outside appeared unchanged from the early aughts. If it had looked like someone was home I might have knocked, asked to come in, told them a few choice stories, but the blinds were drawn and there were no cars in the driveway. I contented myself with a souvenir photo and walked on. When I got back to the hotel I called my sister and told her about everything I'd seen. We didn't talk about Dad; we just talked. We talked for a long time.

April melted into May. Dissertations were defended; the school year juddered and lurched to a close. I shipped a few boxes of books back to Portland, packed a suitcase full of off-season clothes to leave at my in-laws'. Everything else was either donated or thrown away.

For a farewell gift my graduate students got me a bottle of Four Roses and a snakebite kit. I had told them about the trip, of course, and had made a running joke of my total lack of experience with (and likely ineptitude for) camping, which had coalesced into a vocal fear of rattlesnakes, which before long didn't seem to be a joke anymore, just something I was afraid of.

My last day of teaching was May 2, a Wednesday. Since school was over and I wasn't giving any finals, I paid my round of farewell visits and left Hattiesburg that Friday. I left by the same road I'd come in on, I-10, headed east to Pensacola, to spend the week with my in-laws. Over the past year I'd seen quite a bit of them, to the point where Amanda and her sister had taken to joking that I was now the favorite daughter. I sat on their back deck overlooking a canal that feeds into the sound that feeds into the Gulf of Mexico, and filed my final grades from my laptop. I unpacked and repacked the camping gear, took the car in for an oil change.

Pensacola to New Orleans. Amanda's folks come too, in their own car. I pick up Amanda at the airport. We have dinner with her parents downtown.

The next day we get up early, meet Amanda's folks at Cafe Du Monde for beignets and farewells. We are the first people through the door at Central Grocery when it opens. We buy a muffuletta and a bag of Zapp's to share for lunch.

New Orleans to Austin. I drive the first leg. A drizzle as we work our way out of the Quarter and toward I-10 West. Once you get outside the city, the highway turns into a pair of bayou bridges. We pass an exploded big rig on the eastbound side, its cab intact but its whole load gone, the remains of the sidewalls scorched and shredded like the spent shell of a firework. We whip past it so fast it feels like a hallucination, but the dead-stopped eastbound traffic jam snakes on for twenty miles, proof that we saw what we saw. What happened to that truck? What was its cargo and were there fatalities? We never find out. But I can still see it, the blasted-out rig sagging into itself, lightly smoking in gray rain.

Austin to Big Bend. Another early morning, another eight-hour drive. We gas up in Marathon, where the huge blue sky goes gray-black, heralding the storm that catches us out on the two-lane road, where it is flat to the horizon, and wood signs warning of flash floods show the high-water mark above five feet. It seems both impossible and obvious that this whole region was once a shallow sea. When the weather breaks we can see hills and oil pumps. Lightning in the distance. We are headed for a campsite in the Chisos Mountains, our first night out in the open air. We arrive around five and make camp. It goes better than I was expecting. By seven we are walking a short trail that leads to a viewpoint we've heard is an ideal spot to catch the sunset.

Trouble is I'm a little paranoid about what happens if we're caught out here after dark alone. Bears, mountain lions—how long have we been walking? Why haven't we seen anyone else? Am I wearing the wrong shoes? These are sneakers, not my hiking boots. Amanda puts a hand up. "Snake," she says, "in the path." I edge closer, close enough to see it: four or five feet long, pale yellow, basking in the last heat of the day. When he flinches I take off running back the way we came. I don't go far, just far enough to calm down, and Amanda mercifully decides that we won't continue on. Later we'll find out that we were one turn and one hundred feet from the promised viewpoint. As we trudge back toward camp we pass several groups of people, half of them in jeans and flip-flops. Despite my meltdown, this was only ever "hiking" in the loosest sense.

I do not sleep well. I lay awake in my very comfortable sleeping bag on my very comfortable sleeping pad, straining to hear the bears and mountain lions over the sound of my heart in my ears.

A ten-mile hike in the Chisos Basin. We fix a hearty camp breakfast on the Coleman stove that my father-in-law gave us, then set out for the trailhead, our packs loaded up with water, sandwiches, snacks, bug stuff, sunscreen. Unlike the trail on which I melted down yesterday, this is a serious hike. Sun exposure, elevation changes—we even have walking poles! I worry that I'm unprepared, both physically and mentally, which is doubtlessly true, but after last night's poor showing I don't want to embarrass myself a second time, or to ruin this experience for my wife by ruining it for myself. Today is May 15. If he were still alive, today would be Dad's sixty-sixth birthday. I don't want to disappoint him either.

It is a great hike. Happily, I hold my own. I have fun! We appreciate many scenic vistas and are followed for a while by a curious deer. We're back at camp by midday and grab the car to go exploring elsewhere in the park. We drive to the Rio Grande, gaze over into Mexico, hike some more. I know that I will sleep tonight.

Big Bend to Las Cruces. White Sands first thing the next morning, then onward west to the Gila National Forest, where we'll stay at a designated Dark Sky Campground, far enough away from light pollution that you can stargaze with the naked eye. At the campsite, there are concrete pads for setting up telescopes, and you're not allowed to have fires or use flashlights after dark. We set our headlamps to the approved red-light setting, tuck in to a cold supper of charcuterie and crackers. We break the seal on the bottle of Four Roses my students got me. I had been saving it for this. We turn off our headlamps. We spend hours watching the stars come out, tracing the constellations, spotting planets and shooting stars. There are coyotes howling in the distance, a wild and eerie sound, but not (I surprise myself saying this) a frightening one. Amanda wakes me at 3 A.M. and we climb out of the tent. The Milky Way is visible. We stand in the chilly dark and hold each other and stare out into the universe. This could be a dream but it isn't. Or if it is a dream it is a dream come true.

New Mexico to Arizona: the Petrified Forest and the Painted Desert. We arrive at the Grand Canyon in the late afternoon, our first campsite where there isn't a burn ban in effect. Between climate change and the current president, Amanda wasn't kidding when she said we should visit these parks now, because they might not be here in a few years' time. I build the fire and she makes her famous nachos in the cast-iron Dutch oven. In the morning there are elk all around our tent.

South Kaibab Trail, six miles out and back, which is doable, but the elevation gains are what get you. It's equal to walking down—and then back up—the Empire State Building. I get dehydrated and irrational on the return leg. I storm ahead, wanting only for it to be over. Amanda tells me later that I was in such a bad mood she actually started to think about what she'd do if it turned out I'd taken the car and left. But I'm at the trailhead waiting for her, drinking water and becoming human again. Being mad at your pain doesn't make it any less painful. Hot, cramped, sore feet, headache—you can make these things worse by dwelling on them or marginally better by not dwelling on them, but the distance to the end of the path is the same either way. Amanda knows this. She's a runner like Dad was, and it was running that taught her. He knew it too. I am trying to learn it. Will I? Remains to be seen. I did not learn it that day. But perhaps it is enough, for now, to be restored to civility, to a state where I can be a partner, enjoy a vacation, take a walk.

We do take another walk, find another trail, not nearly as steep as South Kaibab, but longer, and we get lost so by the time we find ourselves at a lodge with a restaurant, it is full dark and we've walked fifteen and a half miles—38,430 steps, if you believe the app on my phone. Having climbed the equivalent of 135 flights of stairs. When our beers arrive we weep for joy.

Grand Canyon to Nipton, California. Nipton to Sequoia National Park, then onward to a campsite in Kings Canyon, high in the redwoods, where the air is so damp it takes forty-five minutes to get a fire going. We don't need a fire, but I want one. I want to be able to make one, and to sit by it and sip bourbon and to have this memory of us sitting by a roaring fire sipping bourbon. I don't care how stupid that sounds. I stack and restack the wood, stuff more starter into the nooks and crannies. Eventually, I get what I want.

Yosemite. Amanda and I both came here on family vacations when we were children. My family came in 1991, when I was nine and my sister was three. We visited my aunt Francine, who lived in San Francisco at the time, and then we came out here for a few days. The money for such a trip had not been come by easily or spent lightly; it was important to Dad that we have an experience that justified the expense. We were never a family that bought souvenirs, but here he sprang for a panoramic poster, the famous Ansel Adams photograph that spans from Half Dome to El Capitan. It hung in our house until we sold it in 2004, a reminder of the best family vacation we ever took. (Less often remarked upon was that this was one of the only family vacations we ever took.) Dad loved this place. He loved taking his morning run out here. He loved the hiking and the mountains and the primeval trees and the wonder in his children's eyes. If I could have made the arrangements, if my sister could have joined us, I would have scattered his ashes here.

The next day we've planned a hike through Yosemite Valley. It'll be sixteen and a half miles by the time we're finished, the last and longest hike of the trip. I'm ready for it. As we're finishing breakfast and getting ready to set out, my phone buzzes. It's my friend Joshua. He has texted me a picture of the final paragraph of *Sabbath's Theater*. I open up the *New York Times* app and see that Philip Roth has died.

We leave the park early the next day, skirt around San Francisco, and head for Marin, where we're staying with friends. Tonight is the first night we've slept indoors since Nipton, and before that, Las Cruces.

My friend Peter, one of the three rent-payers at the college house we called Abraham, drives over from Oakland to meet us. He's been a union organizer since the day we graduated, is an expert on state politics and the machinery of city hall. Of all the people I still know (or know of) from my college days, nobody else is living their leftist convictions as fully as he is. The rest of us have made our compromises, or redefined what our convictions are. Some of us went into finance or law or medicine. A few of us are teaching. Some of us sank down from train-hopping and dumpster-diving into working-class alienation and stints in prison. A few of us overdosed or killed ourselves. Peter gets up every day and does what he can for the labor movement. But today he has the day off and we are grateful for the chance to be passengers for a change, so we let him drive us out to Point Reyes Station to visits our friends' bookstore and the Point Reyes Lighthouse.

On the last day of the trip, we take Highway 1 from Marin all the way to where it doglegs inland and tees off in a connection to the 101, which we stay on as far as Crescent City, where we get our last glimpse of the coast before 199 leads us through the Rogue River–Siskiyou National Forest and on to Grants Pass, back in Oregon now, where we pick up I-5, the road that will take us the rest of the way.

Where does this story end? Should it have ended a few pages ago, with my wife and I holding each other beneath the Milky Way? Or earlier still, at the end of the chapter before this one, with the last time I saw Dad? Should it end tomorrow, when we wake up to find that the one thing we left on the backseat of the car (a small backpack full of books) attracted the notice of a junkie who smashed a window to get it, mere hours after the poor Nissan finished a journey that had taken us clear across the country without suffering so much as a scratch or a flat?

Should the book end on June 29, 2018, my thirty-sixth birthday, the same day we close on our house? Should it end July 11, when we move in? On August 11, nearly a year to the day after I drove to Mississippi alone, on a visit back to Nashville where the family is gathered for my cousin Ava's bat mitzvah? The same synagogue where, in August 2019, David Berman's funeral will be held. What if the last thing you saw was me up on the bimah, having been asked by Ava's parents to read a few words from Isaiah to help introduce her *haftorah* portion?

> *And all your children shall be disciples of the Lord,*
> *And great shall be the happiness of your children . . .*

Should the book end on August 28, the first day of the new school year, with me driving down to Salem, Oregon, where I've got a one-year gig as a visiting professor at a liberal arts school? It's not a tenured job—it's not even renewable for a second year—but it's enough to keep me living at home, in my house with my wife, for a while. After that, who knows what will happen? But this is now, and for now all it has to be is enough. And it is enough.

None of these are where the book ends. The book ends the night of May 26, technically very early in the morning on May 27, let's say two hours before the junkie smashes the window. It's 1 A.M., maybe 1:30. I'm driving Dad's car. Amanda's sleeping. The Stones are on the stereo, loud enough to keep me awake, not so loud as to wake her. I am exiting the highway, turning into our neighborhood. The GPS is off because I know where I am. I'm praying for a parking spot right outside our building, and my prayer is answered. I parallel park and cut the engine, and the music cuts with it. In the new silence and stillness, Amanda stirs. Her eyes blink open. And this is where the book ends. It might have ended at other moments, or in other ways, some maybe better or worse, but we'll never know. Life goes on but this story is finished. It ends the moment that we both know we've made it home.

Acknowledgments

Thank you to my mother, my sister, my wife, and my in-laws for their love and support; for crucial insights, tough questions, and endless patience; and for their willingness to be portrayed in these pages.

Thank you to Dorothy Nemetz and John Todd for trusting me with Eli's story. And to Anika Jade, whose story is her own to tell.

Thank you to my readers, whose generosity with their time, attention, and expertise improved this manuscript at every stage of its development: Jami Attenberg, Joshua Cohen, Adam Ross, Eva Talmadge, Adam Wilson, Nell Zink.

Thank you to Noah Ballard, and everyone at Curtis Brown.

Thank you to Caitlin McKenna, Emma Caruso, and everyone at Random House.

Thank you to Literary Arts, the Oregon Literary Fellowships, and the Virginia Center for the Creative Arts, for the provision of time, space, and resources in support of this work.

Thank you to Samuel Nicholson for several things, but

especially for the phone call while I was driving across the Florida Panhandle.

Thank you to Hilary Bell, Jennifer Brewington, Adam Clay, Stephanie DeGooyer, Wes Enzinna, Sarah Gerard, Leslie Jamison, Marie Myung-Ok Lee, David Lehman, Peter Masiak, Amanda Peters, Ed Skoog, and Sam Stephenson.

Thank you to my colleagues and students at the Pratt Institute, Butler University, the University of Southern Mississippi, and Willamette University—all my homes away from home.

ABOUT THE AUTHOR

Justin Taylor is the author of the short-story collections *Everything Here Is the Best Thing Ever* and *Flings,* and the novel *The Gospel of Anarchy.* His work has appeared in *The New Yorker, Harper's,* and *The Sewanee Review,* among other publications. He lives in Portland, Oregon.

justindtaylor.net

Twitter: @my19thcentury

ABOUT THE TYPE

This book was set in Caledonia, a typeface designed in 1939 by W. A. Dwiggins (1880–1956) for the Merganthaler Linotype Company. Its name is the ancient Roman term for Scotland, because the face was intended to have a Scottish-Roman flavor. Caledonia is considered to be a well-proportioned, businesslike face with little contrast between its thick and thin lines.